Down East Netting

S0-AAN-337

Mark P. Smith (on left), superintendent at the net factory, and George Sawyer examine a horse fly net (c. 1900). Courtesy of Kilton Vinal Smith.

Down East
NETTING

A History
and
How-To of Netmaking

Barbara M. Morton

With Illustrations by the Author

DOWN EAST BOOKS

Copyright © 1988 by Barbara Murphy Morton
ISBN 0-89272-231-2
Library of Congress Catalog Card Number 88-51283

Design by Janet Patterson
Printed at Capital City Press, Inc. Montpelier, Vt.

5 4 3 2 1

Down East Books, Camden, Maine

Contents

Acknowledgments

My primary purpose in gathering this material was to pre-serve some of the netting skills that have been rapidly dis-appearing from Maine's coastal towns. I collected informa-tion at random, as one does recipes, and like old recipes they were kept in the back of a drawer. When the time came that I could put notes and patterns together, I realized that some of the most skillful netters were no longer just a few doors away; consequently, many of my thanks are posthumous. My gratitude goes to those who originally showed me how to net: the late Herbert E. Morton, the late Mae Lawry, and the late Flossie Williams. Thanks also go to contemporary netters, such as John E. Morton and Mina Hilding.

I'm also grateful to those who helped me with patterns for this book: Isabel Osgood, Ada Thompson, and Josephine Clayter. The fine points of net mending were clarified by Ronald Walker and Clarence Bennett.

Special thanks are also due to those who gave me nets to copy or photograph: Roger Young, Priscilla Rosen, the late Libby Magnuson, and the Vinalhaven Historical Society.

Introduction

My introduction to netting was in the late fifties, when Maine became my permanent home. So often I would stop at a neighbor's and find all of the family busy at the net stand. Here on the island of Vinalhaven, I found that people netted as confidently and as routinely as they went to the post office to pick up their mail.

An order of netted bags hanging on a hook in a Maine kitchen, the wintry light reflecting the soft sheen in their knotted design, assumes as much beauty as any other handicraft. And the craftsperson, more times than not, is just as pleased as if he or she had just made a cabinet, built a boat, sewn a quilt, or turned out a particularly good batch of bread. There is an undeniable pride in fashioning a viable object from nondescript raw materials. It gives an inner feeling of independence as well as accomplishment; but if the product

Lobster trap heads hanging in the fish house. Charlotte Goodhue photo.

1

has beauty as well as simplicity, it conveys an aura of honesty quite apart from the mass-produced plastic images we so often see today. No matter how it is eventually used or to what stress it is put, there still remains an undefined quality that pleases the beholder. This is true of netting, for how many salt-stained remnants have we all seen that, despite fading and holes beyond repair, still impart an esthetic quality when hung as decoration.

And yet, no netter I have spoken to has ever thought of himself (or herself) as a craftsman. Even though netting is one of the earliest crafts known to mankind, and certainly an important part of the coastal settlements here in America, it is rarely included in craft shows or thought of as a folk art. Nevertheless, the mundane art of netting has contributed to our culture both practically and artistically, for not only were the first fish and animal snares made from netting, the earliest techniques for lacemaking were derived from it as well.

Netting has primitive origins, and any assessment of when the first nets were made is difficult and speculative. From carvings in the Cairo Museum we can see that the Egyptians used nets as early as 3000 B.C. Most materials were so fragile that they soon rotted, leaving no permanent trace for us to unearth. A few relics have been found, some in Switzerland, some in pre-Columbian North America, and some in England and Finland. The fragments found from the Swiss Lake Dwellers show evidence of an incomplete reef knot, and the Finnish fragments utilize a weaver's knot. Further anthropological findings show that the use of this and a similar knot, the Peruvian Knot, was widespread and used by the Peruvian Indians, the Africans, the Chinese, and other fishing communities in remote places of the globe.

The weaver's knot, often referred to as a netter's knot or a sheet bend, and the reef knot are still used in modern netting, but the knot is undergoing changes as ropes and twines are increasingly being made of synthetic materials that make hand-knotting difficult. It is not unusual today to see a netter making the weaver's knot, but, because of the stiffness or slippery finish of some synthetic twines, adding another securing hitch over the weaver's knot, making it a form of double knotting.

Long before man ever thought of making nets, members of the animal kingdom were busy making nets of their own. The caddis larvae survives on plankton trapped in an efficient and symmetrical net, while the spider is constantly spinning a web to catch his prey. Their techniques do not involve a knot, and it has only been in the twentieth century that machines have imitated them by making a knotless net. By the end of the nineteenth century, a mesh cloth could be made by textile machinery. Today, larger nets, beam trawls, seines, or other nets are machine made. The machine can tie the knot similarly to the handmade knot, but as more synthetic fibers are being used, the need to tie is not as pertinent. Some cordage adapts to interweaving, twisting, welding, pasting, or even molding, and knotless netting is being used more frequently.

Even in the face of mass-produced netting it is still essential for a fisherman to have basic skills in the netting arts. Large seines rip, and repairs must often be made at sea. The fisherman who cannot take care of his equipment loses valuable time, money, and equipment. Innovations for diversified nets can only be worked out by knowledgeable application of netting principles, while small nets—lobster heads, for example—are often cheaper made by hand, for they are individually made to fit the size and style of a particular lobsterman's traps. Although all traps may look alike to the visiting Down East tourist, each fisherman has his own idea of what head fishes best for him and what size and how many meshes he wants. Trap heads are usually as individualized as the owners themselves.

Here on Vinalhaven, most of the older people take the ability to net for granted. Many started to net when they were only ten years old, working at the net factory. The factory, built in 1898, is now a garage, and only about half the building remains, nestled against a granite pit at the end of Main Street. There giant looms wove thin colored stays of cotton ribbon, and the lengthy cross-threads of the weft held half-meshes that were gathered by hand to be netted into horse's fly nets, beautiful lacy creations that shimmied when the horse moved, brushing the flies away. The fly nets were finished with loose mesh bonnets, tassels, and netted ear caps.

But netting was done on the island long before the factory was built, the first formal contracts dating back to 1847 when John Carver managed a net company for the American Net and Twine Company. When the Civil War ended,

The Vinalhaven net factory was built in 1897–98 and closed in 1926. On this end of the 2½-story wing was the Main Street door where netters picked up their piecework, usually ear tassels. The small incline at the end of Main Street is still called Net Factory Hill. Courtesy of Carl and Edith Williams.

the "factory girls" paraded jubilantly up and down the Main Street gaily decorated in horse nets. In 1884 many of the nets were handmade, but later some were machine-made, with just the ear tips and tasseling farmed out as piecework. Weekly shipments averaged about 1800 completed nets, but we cannot determine that they were all made on Vinalhaven since piecework was farmed out to neighboring islands as well. Although the large contracts ceased when carriage horses became a thing of the past, netting still related to the fishing industry as well as to a variety of other articles: pickle nets for canneries, pockets for pool tables, basketball goals, tennis nets, landing nets, hurricane lamp covers, placemats, etc. Herbert E. Morton, my father-in-law, received an order for something as unrelated to Maine as an elephant net.

During World War II the need for netters increased when large companies such as General Seafoods could no longer import fishing nets from overseas. Many a living room on Vinalhaven was adorned with a large net rack, and the family spent tedious hours netting the trawls from prickly sisal or coarse manila to keep the American fishing

Pattern for the trawls made on Vinalhaven during World War II. The wings of this Icelandic net are on display at the Mill Race Restaurant.

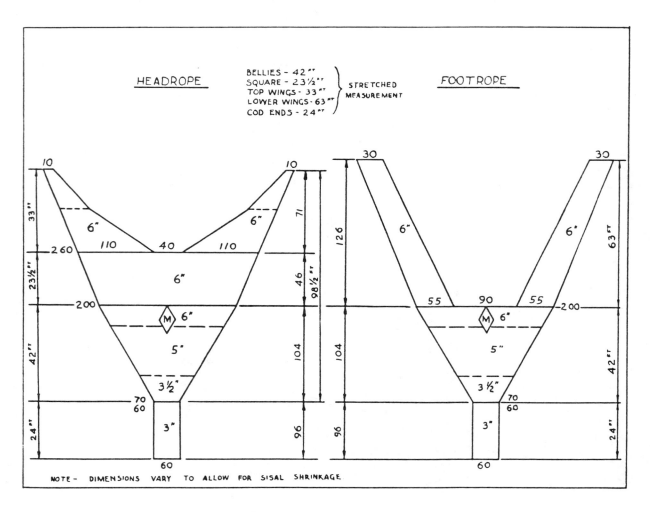

Captain Wilfred Nickerson, Herbert E. Morton, and Etta Morton holding a section of the Icelandic otter trawl sent to Vinalhaven in 1945. Made of sisal, the net measured 52 feet across the entrance as it was being towed. Eliot Elisofon photo, courtesy of Evelyn Greene collection.

fleet supplied. (On display at the Mill Race Restaurant are the wings of an Icelandic otter trawl that was sent over from England during the war for use as a pattern.) My husband's parents, the Herbert E. Mortons, hired the netters and gave them instructions and twine for the nets. Innovations had to be devised. Heavy otter trawls could not be easily flipped over in small living rooms where there was limited space to work the other side. Straight netting is usually done from left to right, the work turned and the next row worked from left to right again. Many netters had to learn how to work in reverse so that the alternate rows could be netted without turning the work. After the war, netting continued but to a limited degree. Orders are still received for a variety of articles, and bait bags and lobster heads are still netted by the older fishermen or their wives, but it is increasingly rare to see a younger person supplement his income by netting, perhaps because there are so many old-timers who are expert—an because the remuneration is minimal.

If you ask Maine netters how they net, the answer will either be by the "old-fashioned way" or the "new-fashioned way." One of the Vinalhaven netters, Rena Johnson, still at it at the age of ninety-five, learned originally to net the old-

Rosa Holmquist at the net stand, late 1940s. Courtesy of Elsie Dunham.

fashioned way, but at age eleven, when she began to get part-time work at the factory, she learned the new-fashioned way. Maine legend tells us that the old way was brought with the early settlers and dates back to Biblical times but the new was adopted in the 1700s. Both methods are described in the text. Most Down East fishermen net the old-fashioned way, but this is suitable only when making relatively large meshes. In this book, the old-fashioned method is indicated where feasible, but all patterns may be made by the new-fashioned method if preferred.

If you talk to a Down Easter, the reference will be to "knitting" and not "netting," and mesh is pronounced "mash." To avoid confusion, the words *netter, netting*, and *mesh* are used in this text.

1 Equipment

The materials needed to start netting are simple and inexpensive. A needle, mesh board, cup hook or nail, and a ball of twine are all that is necessary for the beginner.

The needle, which holds the length of twine, may be homemade from the patterns provided in the text if one cannot be easily purchased. Many craft shops carry plastic netting needles, but the easiest source is either a ship's chandlery or a fishing supply house. Twine manufacturers also carry needles. Listings are in the Appendix.

The mesh board, the gauge that determines the mesh size, may be improvised from any thin wooden slat—a broken yardstick, for example. Many fishermen use their fingers as a gauge, but it is much easier for beginners to use a board. Mesh boards are usually made by the netter.

Synthetic twine, cotton string, or macramé cord are easily obtainable for practice pieces. It is not advisable to use yarn until one is more adept, for knots made in yarn are hard to undo if mistakes happen.

The first loop, or stirrup, is attached to a hook or nail, so have one handy when you are ready to start a practice piece. More detailed descriptions of the needle, mesh board, and foundation attachments (usually a cup hook or nail) are given in the next sections.

The Netting Needle

The needle—sometimes called a shuttle, braiding needle, seine needle, or bobbin—holds the twine [*figure 1-1*]. Its length and width are relative to the size mesh being made. A needle used for fish nets usually ranges from eight to twelve inches long and five-eighths to seven-eighths of an inch wide. The needle should be long enough to hold sufficient twine; a too-short needle must be reloaded more frequently, resulting in an excess of joining knots. The width corresponds to the size of the mesh board or to one leg of the mesh,

Figure 1-1. Parts of the netting needle.

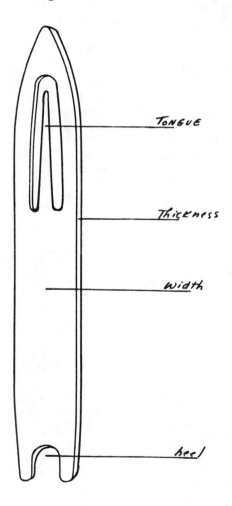

TONGUE

Thickness

Width

heel

7

with the exception that the needle is slightly narrower than the mesh board to allow for the bulk of the twine when the needle is full. If the full needle is wider than the mesh board, it will not pass through the opening easily. The thickness of the needle should be no more than one-eighth inch. It may be purchased from any ship chandlery, from twine companies listed in the Appendix, or from some craft shops.

Up until World War II, netters Down East made their own needles of wood. The old handmade ones were singularly beautiful, an example of an early American art form that is often overlooked. The usual choice of material was whatever hardwood was available: maple, oak, ash, or boxwood. The preferred wood, however, was hornbeam—a hardwood with a grain so fine that the needle looked as though it were made from bone. The netter would sand it with fine paper and then rub with clear oil until it was as white as glass. Netters often had their own block of wood slowly curing in the barn, a piece that had been boiled on the stove for several hours to prevent checking. Today the beauty of netting is in the knots and the design of the nets. The needle has become, like so many other things, a plastic replica that, when worn, can be replaced easily.

Many fishermen still like to make their own needles, so for convenience, some patterns are included here. Select a piece of seasoned hardwood such as oak, birch, cherry, walnut, or maple, not more than a quarter inch thick, and cut out the needle according to the pattern selected [*figure 1-2*]. Sand to one-eighth inch and smooth well so that no rough edges will catch on the twine when netting. Oil lightly with boiled linseed oil. These patterns may be increased or reduced by following the graph. Another method is to solder together two nineteen-inch lengths of #10-gauge wire. One length forms the exterior of the needle and the other length is bent to form the tongue and body [*figure 1-3*].

Figure 1-2. Patterns for netting needles. Each square equals $1/2$ inch.

(1) Sand to $3/16$-inch width, for $1/4$-inch mesh. Used for fine netting. (2) Sand to $7/16$-inch width, for $1/2$-inch mesh. Used for bait bags. (3) Sand to $11/16$-inch width, for $3/4$-inch mesh. Used for bait bags, trap heads, mending nets. (4) Sand to $15/16$ inch, for 1-inch mesh. Most common multipurpose needle for heavier and larger nets.

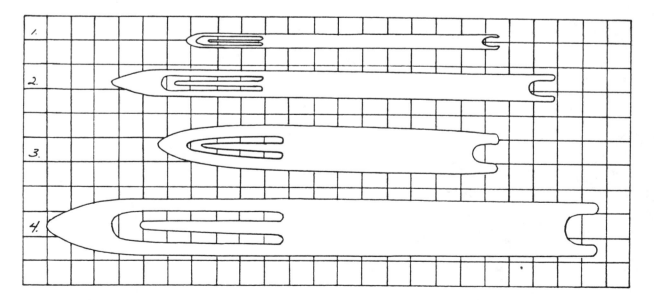

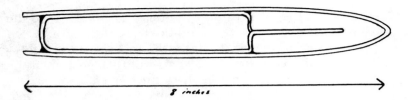

Figure 1-3. A soldered wire needle.

Figure 1-4. Winding the needle.

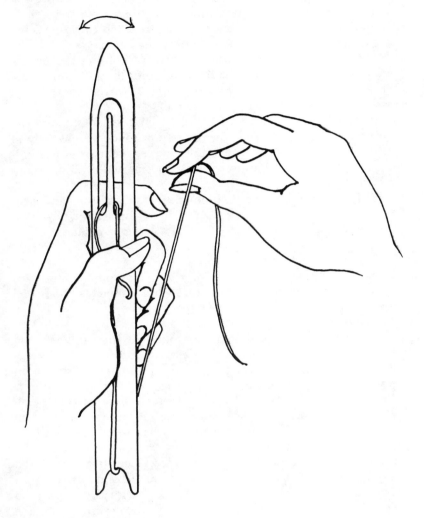

Winding the Needle

Netmaking can begin as soon as the netting needle (or shuttle) is loaded with twine—not so much twine that it will tangle, but not so little that you will have to rewind the needle too often. To wind the needle, follow the steps listed below.

    1. Hold the needle in your left hand with the point up.

    2. With your right hand, lay the twine across the face of the needle about one inch below the base of the tongue and hold it down with your left thumb.

    3. Loop the twine around the tongue from left to right and bring it down on the face of the needle, continuing toward the bottom or heel of the needle.

Figure 1-5. Starting to wind.

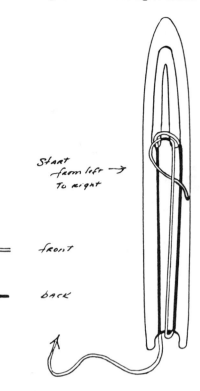

Start from left → To right

front

back

Figure 1-6. Winding with double twine.

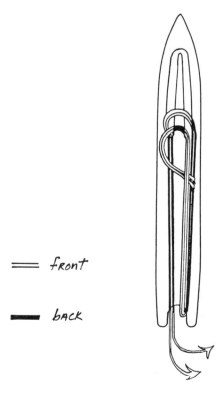

front

bACK

4. Lead the twine under the heel, turning the needle edge-on as you take the twine up the back of the needle. On the back, loop the twine around the tongue from left to right—in other words, away from you. (This will then go around the tongue in the opposite direction from the loop on the front.)

5. With the front of the needle once again facing you, bring the twine from the back under the heel and toward the front again. Release your thumb from the face of the needle and loop the twine around the tongue from left to right, down the front, and under the heel again to the back.

6. Continue in this manner, always holding the needle upright. The twine is loaded first on the front and then on the back, but do not turn the needle completely over, for this will cause a kink in the twine (see below).

7. When no more twine will fit on the tongue, cut the twine from the ball. Your needle is now loaded and ready to use. (If you are using synthetic twine, sever it from the ball by burning rather than cutting it; the melted stub prevents raveling.)

To wind the needle with double twine, use the same procedure, holding two strands of twine (from separate balls) together and treating them as if they were one strand.

Eliminating Kinks

Even though loading a needle is relatively simple, there are times when multiple twists occur, which impedes the speed and uniformity of netting. These may be eliminated in a couple of ways.

Experienced netters recommend "winding with the sun." I was reminded of that rule when my first needle was full of kinks. I was told to face south and imagine the sun on my left hand in the morning and my right hand at night. Twine is usually twisted and put on a spool in this same clockwise manner. As a general rule, if the twine is taken off the spool from left to right, unwanted kinks will be avoided. If kinking persists, check to see if the twine is coming off the spool in the manner described. If not, turn the spool over so that the twine does come off from left to right. This simple procedure should be all that is needed to proceed smoothly, but unfortunately this is not always true, for some of the modern twines seem to have spontaneous twists all their own. Even with these offbeat spools, however, the twists will be reduced if you wind with the sun. (Placing the spool in an empty coffee can will prevent it from rolling away.)

The needle should be wound as directed from left to right and back to the left; it should not be turned completely around. If the twine is connected to the spool, turning the needle over would normally bring on added twists. There are exceptions to this rule, such as when the spool itself has been improperly wound by the manufacturer. In this case, revolving the needle clockwise until the kinks have been released sometimes helps.

If twists appear as you wind, drop the needle toward the

floor and let it hang. Since the twine is caught around the tongue, the needle will not unwind more than a few turns. Let the needle hang until the twists spin away and then proceed to wind in the proper manner.

Another simple way to eliminate twists is to fill the needle, kinks and all, then cut the twine. Rewind, working out the twists as the twine comes through your fingers. Then use this measurement for subsequent needles. This method is time-consuming, but it is less confusing for beginners.

The Mesh Board

The gauge that determines the size of the netted mesh and assures its uniformity is the mesh board, so, logically enough, the size of the board depends on the desired size of the mesh. Experienced netters can often control the mesh size as they work by measuring on their fingers, but the average netter finds it simpler to use a board. In some areas the board is called a stick or gauge, but Down East it is called a mesh board. It is usually made from wood, although modern boards are made from a variety of materials, including plexiglass.

Many mesh boards are only thin rectangular strips, and these seem to serve the purpose adequately, but the preferred board is almond-shaped in cross-section, with the rounded side on the base and the thin point on the top as used. The point and the beginning arc of the almond serve as a resting place for the line of knots that is being formed, and this facilitates even tying of rows of meshes.

The length of the board can vary, usually running from three to six inches. The important measurement is the circumference around the board, whether it be flat-sided or almond shaped. The measurement around the board should be one half of the circumference of the desired mesh size.

An easy way to determine what size board to use is to take a single mesh and pull it together, keeping it taut from the top knot to the bottom knot. Measure the stretch line from the middle of the top knot to the bottom knot. This length will be the desired circumference of the board. If you are making your own board and want a certain mesh size, measure the stretch line from the top to bottom knot with a thin strip of paper. Using this paper as a guide or pattern, cut out the mesh board from wood or the desired material slightly larger than the size needed. Sand the board smoothly until the approximate measurement is reached. Wrap the pattern around the width of the board and when the ends butt, the board will be the correct size.

To a netter, the quality of the board is as important as the needle, and the boards used by the old netters were carefully cut, planed, and sanded. They were made from a variety of woods, such as maple, oak, ash, hickory, or sometimes of ivory. In mid-coast Maine, where shipping was still a major industry at the turn of the century, it was always

Figure 1-7. Mesh boards.

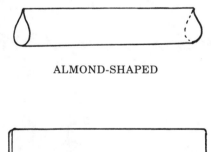

ALMOND-SHAPED

RECTANGULAR

Figure 1-8. Fishermen's mesh measurements.

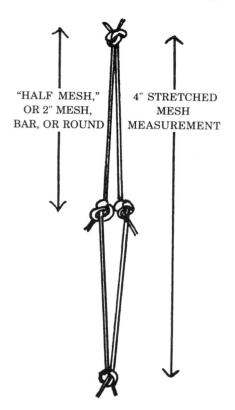

"HALF MESH," OR 2" MESH, BAR, OR ROUND

4" STRETCHED MESH MEASUREMENT

hoped that a barque making an African or South American run would return with a cargo that contained some lignum vitae, a durable wood that shipbuilders used to make the sheaves for blocks. This hard, dense wood never seemed to wear. Mesh boards made from pine or even the preferred hardwoods eventually wore down, developing a swayback groove. This often deeply hollowed groove changed the uniform measurement of the mesh. Some old boards found in attics are hollowed out as much as a quarter inch off the intended measure. Mesh boards made of lignum vitae lasted a netters' lifetime.

Mesh Size and Measurement

Terminology for determining mesh size is confusing, for the methods of measuring vary in the different fishing communities of the world. Some fishermen measure one side of the diamond, referring to this as a leg, bar, square, or round. If an example measured two inches, it would be called a two-inch-square mesh. Down East this is called a "half-mesh." Others would measure two sides of this same square or diamond and call it a four-inch measure, while some measure all four sides and call it an eight-inch mesh.

Yet another method is to stretch the mesh to a narrow diamond shape [*figure 1-8*] and measure the distance between the centers of the top and bottom knots. A two-inch-square mesh, as determined by the first method, would now be a four-inch stretched mesh. English authorities measure this size by slipping a four-inch flat gauge through the mesh when wet. In Maine, some controversy has arisen when wardens check that shrimp nets measure legal mesh size, for the method used is essentially the same as the English. Fishermen feel that that the shrinkage or the elasticity of the twine after wear affects the ultimate mesh size, often making the net appear illegal.

The generally accepted method among Maine coast fishermen is to pull the mesh together. The distance from the middle of the top knot to the bottom knot is considered the mesh size. Mesh sizes mentioned in this text have been measured by this method and are referred to as a "stretched mesh."

Twines and Their Terminology

Until the early 1950s, twines were made from vegetable fibers: cotton from seed pods, sisal and manila from leaves, or linen and hemp from the bast fibers of stems. In Maine, the lighter and smaller nets were made from cotton and the heavier nets—otter trawls, for example—were made from sisal.

Once the nets were wet, they rotted quickly. The rotting process stopped only when they were completely dry. On sunny, windy days, yards of nets were spread to dry in the open fields, and one could smell the tar pots heating over open fires as fishermen, greased to their shoulders, dipped their nets in an attempt to preserve them.

Preservatives did not work well. Tar made a net stiffer, heavier, and helped prevent abrasion, but it did not penetrate the fibers unless the twine was left in the tar for three hours at a temperature above 180 degrees (cotton begins to scorch at 220 degrees). Some fishermen today still prefer tarred nets, and, for an additional cost, twine may be purchased already tarred.

Another popular preserving method was "cutching," using a tanning solution, but for it to be effective the nets had to be redipped in about six days. Chemicals such as potassium bichromate, copper sulphate, etc., were tried, and although they helped to a degree, none of these preserved the net for any appreciable length of time.

Synthetic materials, especially nylon, polyethylene, and polypropylene, came into their own as netting materials in the early fifties. The important characteristic of these twines is that they do not rot.

The synthetics are a mixed blessing, though, when one considers their ecological consequences. Nets made of vegetable fibers decompose, releasing inorganic nutrients such as the phosphorus, nitrogen and potassium so important for plant growth. The synthetic nets, and now wire traps, not only do not rot but continue to fish even when lost to the sea. This was dramatically illustrated on television when gill nets caught on the wreckage of the *Andrea Doria* were shown endlessly ghost fishing on the ocean bottom.

Even though synthetics resist bacteria and mildew, they do react to sunlight, and therefore have a longer life span if they are dyed. This step is better left to the manufacturer's chemist, who knows what dyes are best for specific synthetic compounds. Fish slime, chlorine, some oils, and excessive heat damage synthetics, and nets should be rinsed and stored when not in use.

The netting instructions in this text designate the type and size of twine usually used in coastal Maine, but when purchasing twine for other nets you may find that some of the labeling used by manufacturers is difficult to understand because netmaking terminology is not universally consistent and specifications can vary from one manufacturer to another. A few terms are defined here so that you may find the best material for your own netting projects.

Let's start briefly with cotton twine. A *hank* of cotton is 840 yards of a single strand, and a *skein* or *ball* has as many hanks in it as it takes to make a pound. The size of the twine has a number: the lower the number, the thicker the twine. If one multiplies the size by 840 the result will be the yardage in a pound.

Ply refers to the number of strands that are twisted to make the twine. For example, 2-ply would have two strands twisted together. This twisting shortens the yardage; therefore, one must divide the estimated yardage by the ply number and allow for about a 5% loss in twisting. Let's say that you have a pound of #24 that is 3-ply. Multiply 24 by 840 and the answer is 20,160. Divide that figure by 3 (for the ply), subtract 5% for loss in twisting, and the final figure is 6,505 yards. Twine is often labeled with a number, a diagonal line, and then a second number. The first number is the size, the second is the ply.

Cotton twine also may be purchased from some nylon-twine companies, and the Handweavers Guild of America, Inc., issues a catalog of current weaving suppliers. (The guild's address is listed in the appendix.) Charts A and B show specifications for cotton twine and cotton trot line available from the Nylon Net Company.

Synthetics do not lend themselves to this simple formula, and their yardage is usually listed on the ball. Heading twine is used on the New England coast for making lobster trap heads and bait bags and for mending, etc. It comes in a variety of thicknesses, but the label numbers (#550, #750, or #1000) refer only to the yardage per pound. The lower the number, the thicker the twine. Down East fishermen learn from experience what size of twine to use for a particular job.

Other twines are listed according to their diameter, approximate feet per pound, and approximate break test. Chart C is an example of how the specifications are usually listed.

Ready-made nets have three main divisions: knotless,

Chart A: Cotton Cable Cord / Seine Twine Specifications

(Courtesy of Nylon Net Company, Memphis, Tenn.)

TWINE SIZE NO.	APROXIMATE DIAMETER (IN.)	APROXIMATE FT. PER LB.	APPROXIMATE BREAK TEST (LBS.)
15	.051	860	30
18	.058	806	35
21	.065	716	40
36	.085	430	70

Chart B: Cotton Trot Line Specifications

(Courtesy of Nylon Net Company, Memphis, Tenn.)

TWINE SIZE NO.	APPROXIMATE DIAMETER (IN.)	APPROXIMATE FT. PER LB.	APPROXIMATE BREAK TEST (LBS.)
0	$1/8$	179	150
1	$5/32$	176	175

Chart C: Specifications for Nylon Twine

(Courtesy of Nylon Net Company, Memphis, Tenn.)

TWINE SIZE	REGULAR NYLON TWINE		TWISTED NYLON TWINE		
	BREAK TEST (APPROX.)	FT. PER LB. (APPROX.)	DIAMETER (IN.) (APPROXIMATE)	BREAK TEST (APPROX.)	FT. PER LB. (APPROX.)
#3	20 lbs.	9610			
#4	29	6085			
#5	48	4618			
#6	60	3746	.031	50	3804
#7	73	3025			
#9	91	2195	.042	80	2304
#12	106	1782	.046	100	1740
#15	153	1447	.051	120	1404
#18	203	1092	.058	160	1104
#21	253	856	.065	200	864
#24	297	685	.073	240	744
#30	268	635	.078	280	624
#36	352	488	.085	320	540
#42	424	378	.093	360	459
#48	459	368	.103	440	375
#54	473	328			
#60	618	285	.116	560	300
#72	647	249	.125	640	261
#84	884	208			
#96	1011	179	.158	920	174
#120	1130	146	.170	1120	138

twisted, and braided, and the type desired should be specified when ordering. The knotless nets have several advantages, the primary ones being that they are lighter and less bulky. The knot is usually replaced by a twist, braid, or a series of interlocking bars and joints.

Definitions follow that are helpful in ordering specific types of twine.

Netting yarn: any textile material that can be used for fishing nets.

Strand or *single yarn:* one thread only.

Netting twine: two or more threads that have been twisted in one operation.

Cabled netting twine: twisted netting twines combined by further twisting.

Braided netting twine: manufactured by braiding rather than twisting the strands.

2 Getting Started

Planning the Net

Quite often a netter will want to make an original design and not use a pattern. Once the mesh size is decided, one may estimate how many meshes are needed for the project. To do this, one leg or bar of the mesh is used as a guide. As an example, we'll assume that the desired net will measure thirty-six inches on a side.

Diamond-shaped nets are determined by measuring the diagonal of the mesh and dividing it into the width or length of the desired size net. For example, if one leg of the mesh is one-half inch, the diagonal is eleven sixteenths, and the needed meshes for thirty-six inches would be fifty-one. (This is assuming that the mesh is in the shape of a forty-five-degree diamond. Fishing nets are usually not pulled tightly across, but hang in an elongated fashion. This is compensated by adding 25 percent more meshes to the width and subtracting 15 percent from the length. Thus, the same three-foot-wide net made for fishing would need sixty-four meshes across and forty-one meshes down.)

Refer to Chart D to determine these numbers, bearing in mind that the figures are only approximations, for the size of the twine and the individual knot affects the number of meshes.

A square-meshed net, which has parallel sides, is less complicated to calculate. Simply divide one side of a mesh into the desired width or length for the finished net. A net thirty-six inches long that has a mesh measuring half an inch would need approximately seventy-two meshes across and seventy-two meshes down, minus the approximate width of the twine.

To determine the amount of meshes needed in a tubular net, simply divide the circumference by the diagonal of the mesh, adding 25 percent to the result if the mesh is not to be stretched tightly.

16

Chart D: Dimensions for a 36-Inch Net

| | DIAMOND-SHAPED NET | | ELONGATED DIAMOND | |
MESH SIZE	DIAGONAL	NO. OF MESHES LENGTH & WIDTH	NO. OF MESHES FOR LENGTH	NO. OF MESHES FOR WIDTH
1/2"	1 1/16"	51	41	64
3/4"	1 1/16"	33	24	41
1"	1 7/16"	25	21	34
1 1/4"	1 3/4"	20	18	27
1 1/2"	2 1/8"	17	15	20
1 3/4"	2 1/2"	14 1/2	13	18
2"	2 13/16"	13	11	16
2 1/2"	3 9/16"	10	8 1/2	13
3"	4 1/4"	8 1/2	7	10

Adapted from *Netmaking,* by P.W. Blandford.

The Foundation Attachment

The netting knot is made by tying into a loop or mesh from the preceding row. This necessitates a foundation loop or series of loops from which to begin. Because netmaking requires strong tugs to obtain even knots, the foundation loop must be held by something solid so the knots can be firmly pulled into place. For something small, such as a lobster-pot head or a bait bag, a good-sized cup hook placed in a wall slightly above chest level will be adequate. For larger netting that requires a series of beginning loops, strong hooks or nails placed in a wall at the required distance apart hold a headrope, dowel, or in the case of a beam trawl, a half-inch pipe called a net rack. This might hold several yards of starting loops.

When making small pieces of netting, most Down Easters use a net stand. This is a rectangular frame with an open box at the bottom and an open box at the top, each a foot square. The boxes, three inches deep, are used to hold extra needles and twine. The sides of the stand are open, allowing comfortable space for the knees or a footrest. Four supporting corner posts, thirty inches high, hold the stand together. The posts extend an inch below the bottom box to form legs, and protrude an inch or more at the top. A nail or hook is inserted in each post at the top. The netter sits by the stand and works from one of the corner hooks, utilizing spare hooks to hang the finished work. Sometimes a group of netters spending a sociable afternoon will share the same stand. The net stand, like the needle and mesh board, is functional, and all stands are essentially the same design. Some are just old boards nailed together enough to make do, while others are painted or highly varnished. One net stand I have seen had

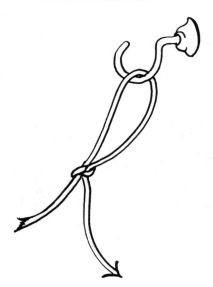

Figure 2-1. A cup hook attached to the wall just above chest level (when seated) makes a convenient foundation attachment.

Figure 2-2. Netting suspended from a pipe or dowel.

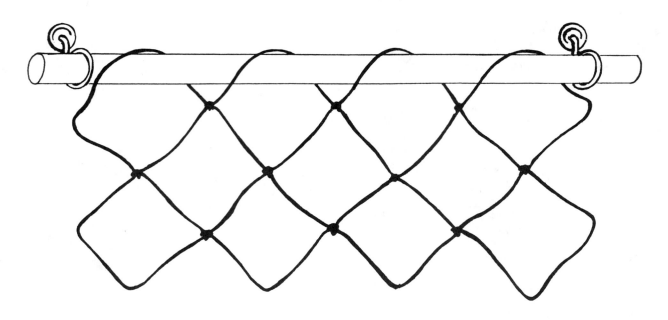

Figure 2-3. A simply constructed net stand.

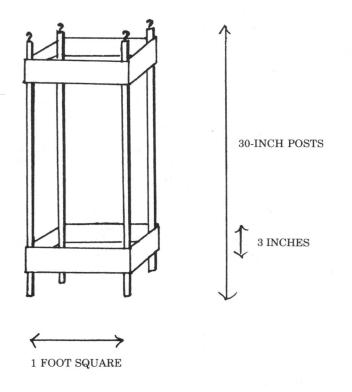

30-INCH POSTS

3 INCHES

1 FOOT SQUARE

Working around the net stand can be a social occasion. Here Dot Calderwood, Mina Hildings, and Leatrice Hildings work on trap heads. Charlotte Goodhue photo.

a drawer for needles, gauges, and patterns, another had a granite block in the bottom to keep it from creeping, while still another had a bed at the base for the family cat.

Net stands, hand-crafted, have various measurements, but the measurements given above are perhaps the most common. To make a simple net-stand, refer to the diagram, sanding all surfaces well so the twine will not catch as you work. Cabinetmakers have made net stands that are things of beauty, but essentially they are utilitarian.

Taking Up with the Chain Start

Meshes are needed to start a net, for the netting knot (the weaver's knot, also called sheet bend) is worked into the mesh above, so I will begin with instructions on how to make the foundation meshes and then discuss how to knot into those starting meshes to form the fabric of the net. However, it is a chicken-and-egg situation, in a way, for one must know how to tie a sheet bend in order to form that first mesh! Since I have to start somewhere, I'll begin with the foundation mesh, but I *strongly recommend* that you first read ahead to the section called "Netting the Old-Fashioned Way" (pages 24 to 27) before actually beginning your project.

Down East, making the foundation meshes is called "taking up." There are several ways of doing this, but a popular method is the chain start. Perhaps it is because so many

Figure 2-4. Taking up
with the chain start.

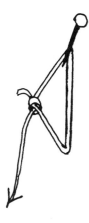

of the lobster heads are started this way that Maine people learn this method first from necessity. The chain is worked down and then turned sideways to form the top of the net.

1. Make a small overhand knot (like step 1 of tying a shoelace) on the end of the twine.

2. Above the end knot make a loop twice the size of the mesh board on the end of the twine. This may be done by wrapping the twine twice around the mesh board for accurate measure and securing that loop with a weaver's knot (sheet bend) as shown on pages 24 to 27.

3. Hang the loop on a hook or nail and turn the loop so that the knot is in the middle of the left side. This is the starting mesh. The distance from the side knot to the top of the loop or to the base of the loop should be the size of your mesh board.

4. Hold the mesh board at the bottom of the loop, pull the twine in front of the mesh board, up in back of the board, and through the above mesh, coming from back to front. Pull the twine so that it is evenly wound around the board and is resting through the loop at the top of the board. Make a weaver's knot by the old-fashioned method, as in step 2 above.

5. Continue downward in this manner until there are twice the number of knots as the number of meshes desired. For example, twenty knots will give ten meshes. As you make the chain, keep the twine taut. Notice that each time a mesh is formed, it falls on the opposite side—first on the right and then on the left. Netting it up on the same side puts a twist in the chain. The first two or three loops will be difficult to pick up without turning over the chain, but as one continues (always holding the chain taut), turning it will no longer be necessary.

6. When all the knots are made (twice as many as the desired number of meshes), pick up the meshes. Take only the left side. Put your thumb down in the first mesh, up in the second, down in the third and so on until all of the left-sided meshes are on your thumb. Check the protruding right-hand meshes. If you have made twenty knots, there should be ten meshes.

7. Make a stirrup by doubling a piece of twine about twelve inches long and knotting the ends together. Insert the stirrup into the meshes that were on your thumb, straighten out the right-hand meshes, which will now be on the bottom, and hang both ends of the stirrup on a hook.

8. Net across from left to right. This will be the third row. When you are finished with a row, the work will easily flip over on the stirrup so that the next row will also be worked from left to right.

If the net being made is large, the picked up meshes may be put on a rod instead of a stirrup. Secure the rod so that the work remains taut and flat. To continue working from left to right, the rod must be turned at the end of each row, or the piece worked alternately from both sides of the rod, or the alternate rows worked in reverse.

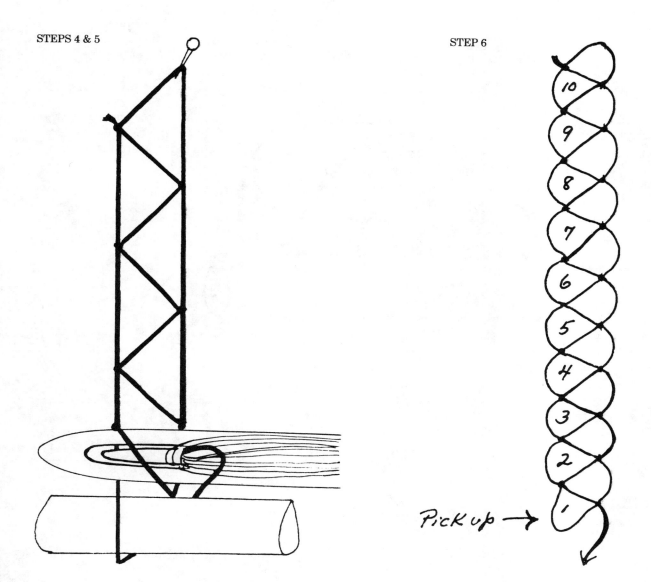

Pick up →

Taking Up with a Foundation Loop

This beginning is more versatile than other methods, for after the meshes are taken up, the loop may be pulled together as the start of a circular net or it may be opened to begin a flat net. Two of the practice pieces shown later, the bait bag and the thermos cover, are examples of this method. In this case, the loops formed differ from the chain start in that half instead of whole meshes are being formed.

In figure 2-5, old-fashioned netting is shown for clarity. Those who work in new-fashioned netting usually start this way too.

1. Tie a length of twine together in the same manner as described for making a stirrup in step 7 above: a simple overhand knot connecting the two ends. The length of the

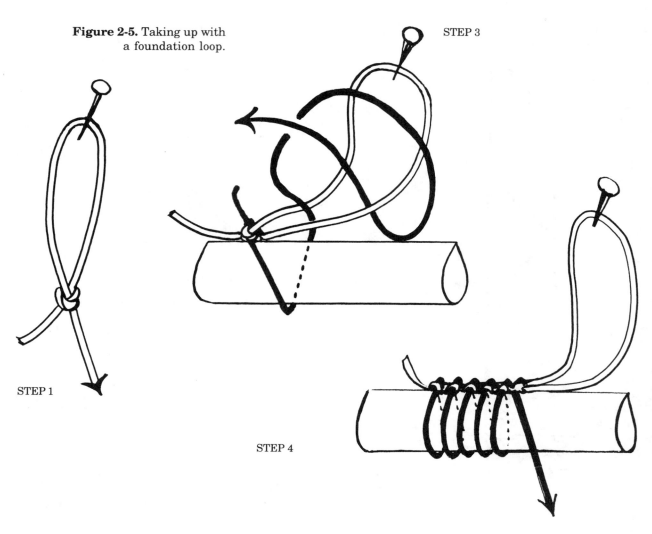

Figure 2-5. Taking up with a foundation loop.

STEP 3

STEP 1

STEP 4

twine depends on the piece of netting, but two feet of twine usually is plenty for a small net. Hang the loop on a hook.

2. Knot the lead twine to the end of the loop just under the original knot. (This step is omitted in some nets and the loop is made in the end of the working twine. In the bait bag pattern, the twine must be tied on separately, for the foundation loop is later incorporated as a free drawstring.)

3. Make a weaver's knot by going around the mesh board from front to back and up *through* the foundation loop. Make a swing to the left, above, and to the right as in regular netting and go under *both* strands.

4. Continue making knots adjacent to each other until the number of meshes needed for the width of the net is reached. The foundation loop will pull down along the top of the mesh board.

5. Count the number of knots on the board and you will notice that there will be one more knot than the number of loops on the board. The meshes are determined by the knots rather than the loops.

6. Turn the work and net the next row, continuing until

the desired length is reached. (Special directions are given in a later chapter, "Circular and Tubular Netting," for those variations.)

7. When the length has been reached, the foundation loop is removed. The work will open up flat, and the top row netted on the foundation loop will appear as a serrated edge. The original knots made on the foundation loop will pull out when the loop is removed, and for this reason the half-meshes originally made will be slightly larger than those in the body of the net. To compensate, the first meshes may be made on a smaller board, or the serrated edge turned onto itself to take up the slack when an attaching line is strung through the upper meshes.

Taking Up with the Clove Hitch

The third method of taking up is with the clove hitch. This may be done on a rod or headrope.

1. Start by tying the end of the twine with an overhand knot to secure it.

2. Leave enough slack in the twine to be equal to a half-mesh and make a clove hitch on the rod.

3. The clove hitch is two half-hitches, each made the same way, either both under or both over the rod. Start by putting the needle under and behind the rod, around and up and to the front. Go down under the twine left from the previous half-mesh. Continue up again, behind the rod, and down under the cord left between the two half-hitches [see figure 2-6].

4. Pull to tighten.

5. Leave cord sufficient for another half-mesh and make another clove hitch.

6. Repeat, making enough clove hitches to support the required number of half-meshes [figure 2-7].

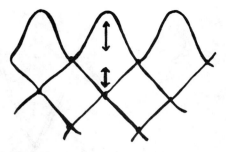

THE FIRST ROW OF MESHES WILL BE SLIGHTLY LARGER THAN THE REST.

TURNING THE TOP LOOPS AS THEY ARE STRUNG ONTO A LINE (STEP 7).

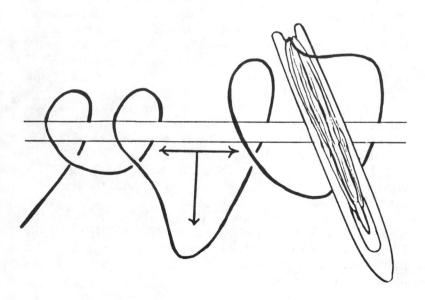

Figure 2-6. Taking up with clove hitches worked on a headrope. The distance between hitches should be equal to the desired width of meshes. Length of the starting loops should be equal to one-half mesh.

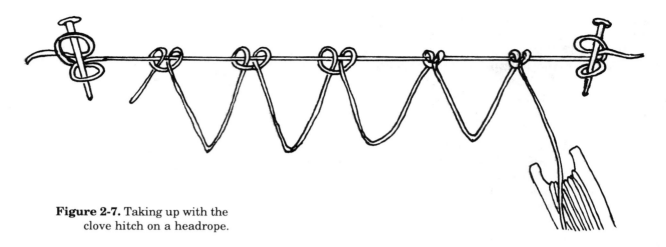

Figure 2-7. Taking up with the clove hitch on a headrope.

Netting the Old-Fashioned Way

The "old-fashioned" way of netting differs from the "new-fashioned" way in that the needle is shuttled *under* the strands of the upper mesh. The old-fashioned method has a definite advantage for certain nets. A torn net, such as a beam trawl, may be prepared for mending much more quickly if it has been netted in the old-fashioned way because the knots are easier to snap out. This method has the disadvantage of being awkward for very fine work. Most of the fishermen on the island of Vinalhaven net the old-fashioned way unless they are netting the very small mesh needed for eel nozzles or some bait bags.

(Note: For all patterns in this book where the old-fashioned netting method is specified, the new-fashioned method may be substituted.)

The netting knot (weaver's knot or sheet bend) is tied to a series of loops or meshes from the previous row and worked from left to right. To begin, one needs a series of these loops or meshes as a foundation. For a practice piece, set these up on a rod between clove hitches, as described above. The loops, in this case, will appear in the finished piece as half of the first mesh row, and this will be apparent as the work continues. Other methods for starting out are described earlier: "Taking Up with the Chain Start" (page 19) and "Taking Up with a Foundation Loop" (page 21).

Wind the needle with medium to heavy twine—so you can see the knot more easily as you make it for the first time —and use a fairly large mesh board (three inches is fine) so that the mesh is a good size.

1. Secure a rod between two nails, hanging it far enough away from the wall so that you can pull the twine behind the rod easily when taking up.

2. Tie an overhand knot in the end of the lead twine and make a clove hitch as described in "Taking Up with the Clove Hitch," page 23. Make a loop equivalent to half of a mesh between each hitch. Using the mesh board, make six loops for a practice piece.

3. Turn the rod so that you will be working from the left and secure the rod between the two hooks again.

4. Hold the mesh board in the left hand under the first loop.

5. Bring the twine down over the front of the board, continuing under and upward toward the loop above on the rod. Enter the loop from behind and bring the working twine forward and down.

6. Adjust the twine by pulling on the needle so that the loop of the upper half-mesh fits snugly on the top of the mesh board [*figure 2-8*].

7. Press down on the board with the left forefinger, holding the loop in position. Make a large swing with the needle to the left and up, continuing to the right over the strands of the upper half-mesh.

8. Now bring the needle under the two strands of the upper half-mesh, from the right toward the left, passing over the arc made by the swinging motion [*figure 2-9*].

9. Pull the twine down tightly to where the forefinger is pressed and gently squeeze the end of the loop as the twine forms a tight knot [*figures 2-10 and 2-11*]. This last motion ensures that the knot will form on the top of the preceding mesh. If, as you pull, the twine slips under the bottom of the upper mesh, the knot will not hold [*see figure 2-12*]. Continue across the meshes until the row is complete.

10. Flip the rod over so that you are again working from left to right. Bring the twine down under the mesh board and up into the loop as you did for the previous row.

11. Continue for six rows, make an overhand knot in the lead twine adjacent to the last weaver's knot, and cut off the twine.

Remove the piece from the rod and check to make sure all the knots are on top of the lower part of the preceding mesh. This is only a practice piece and may be discarded, or

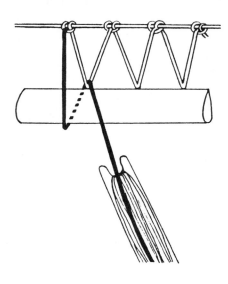

Figure 2-8. Old-fashioned netting.

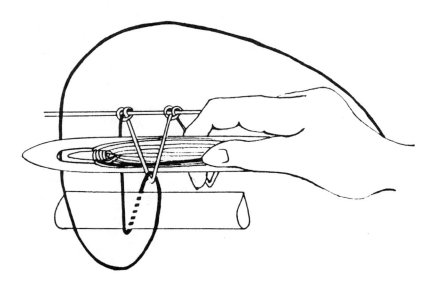

Figure 2-9. Old-fashioned netting.

Figure 2-10. Pinching the mesh as the knot is tightened.

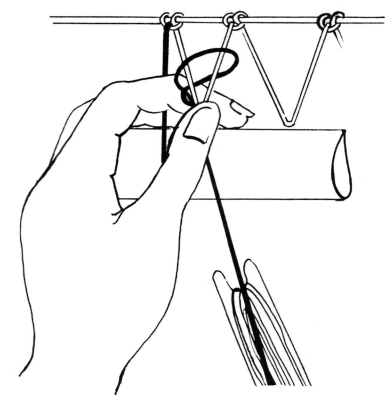

Figure 2-11. Appearance of the knot as it is being pulled tight.

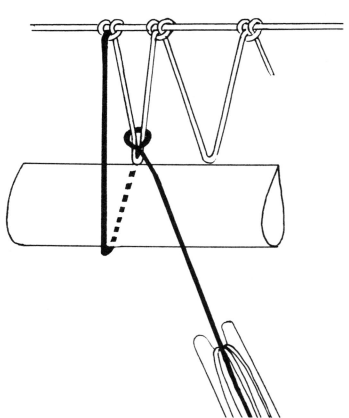

if you are not sure of the knot, tie on the twine, start from the left, and practice a few more rows.

Netting the New-Fashioned Way

New-fashioned netting is used for fine work, where the old-fashioned method would not be practical. Although the needle picks up the mesh, it does not go behind the strands as it does in old-fashioned netting, making very fine meshes possible without contending with the added bulk of the needle. It makes a tighter knot than does the old-fashioned method, as well as lending itself to a variety of nets in need of a secure tie.

1. Hold the mesh board between the thumb and forefinger of the left hand. The middle, fourth, and little finger are dropped below the board.

2. Form an arc by swinging the working twine to the left and then to the right, as one does in making the knot the old-fashioned way, but hold the arc in place with the left *thumb* and bring the twine back down *behind* the mesh board and around the left little finger [*see figure 2-13*].

3. Now bring the needle under the first loop made when the twine was originally put around the middle and fourth fingers [*figure 2-14, #1*], then over the lower end of the loop that was held by the thumb [*#2*], coming up behind the mesh board, up through the above mesh from the back [*#3*], and

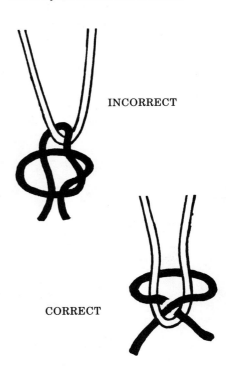

Figure 2-12. Appearance of knot made by old-fashioned method.

INCORRECT

CORRECT

Figure 2-13. New-fashioned netting. Starting the knot.

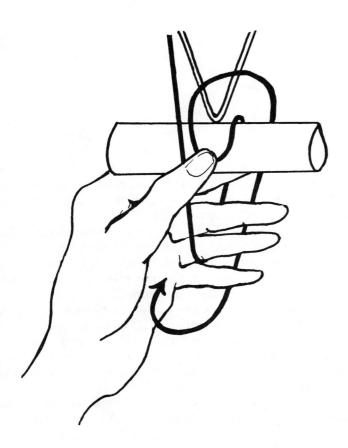

Figure 2-14. (1) Twine under; (2) twine over; (3) twine under; (4) twine over.

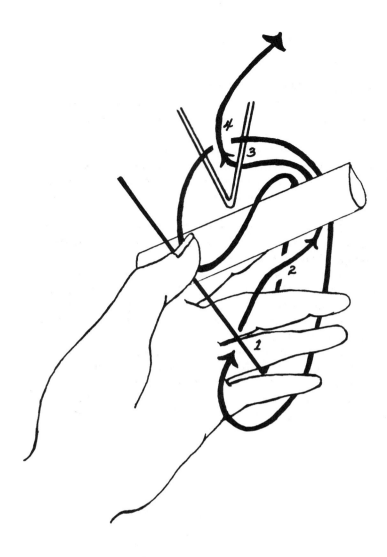

over the top of the arc [*#4*] that has been anchored by the thumb. (As you get into the swing of it, remember that the sequence is: under, over, under, and over.)

4. Pull the knot down on the mesh board. When doing this last step, pull away the third and fourth fingers, maintaining tension on the loop still caught on the little finger [*figure 2-15*]. As the knot comes into place, remove the little finger and pull the knot tight to secure it.

To make a practice piece in new-fashioned netting, see the above directions for starting on a foundation loop, take up fourteen meshes on a mesh board with medium twine, and net down ten rows. Instead of discarding this practice piece, net it together using the method described for the Glass Float Cover (page 43). You now have a bait bag or float cover. If your first effort comes out with some mistakes, ignore them and fill the bag with suet for the birds—then try again.

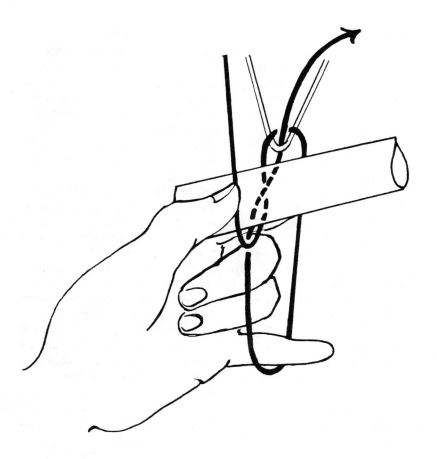

Figure 2-15. Release third and fourth fingers.

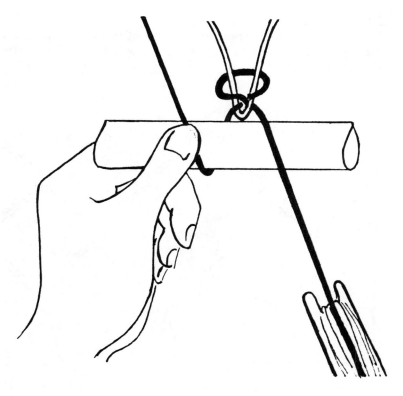

Figure 2-16. Pulling the knot tight.

Figure 2-17. Adding a second mesh.

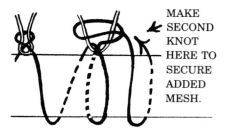

MAKE SECOND KNOT HERE TO SECURE ADDED MESH.

Figure 2-18. Continue netting into next mesh as usual.

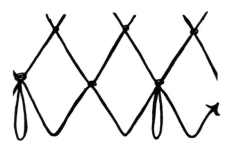

Widening

Widening is the local Maine term for increasing the size of the net by adding more meshes. Many seafarers refer to widening as "creasing." When enlarging a net, it is important to keep in mind the ultimate shape of the net desired. Adding one extra mesh at the end of each successive row will provide a net that slants at approximately a 45-degree angle. Sometimes it is desirable to increase in the middle of the net, but it usually makes a more uniform piece if an increase is not directly under the preceding one.

To increase, make a mesh by the normal procedure, then take the twine and go around the board again, but instead of coming up in the next loop above, tie onto the knot formed by the mesh just made. Continue netting into the next mesh in the normal fashion. [*See figures 2-17 and 2-18.*]

A second method is to make a false mesh. The advantage to this method is that the mesh may be added as one nets along, particularly if one has overlooked adding the extra mesh in the row above by the other method. After making a regular mesh, go around the mesh board again, but instead of tying into the next loop, go to the knot above (letting the twine flow free enough to keep the rows even) and tie into that knot [*figure 2-19*]. Bring the end down even with the row of knots being made. There will be two strands, one the strand being led up, and the other the strand coming down. Knot these two strands together evenly with the current row of knots. Go around the mesh board to make the next loop and continue netting in the usual manner. [*See figure 2-20.*]

Narrowing

Narrowing means decreasing the size of the net (also called "bating"). The same rule applies as for widening; that is, the narrowing should be done evenly so as not to distort the net.

Figure 2-19. Making a false mesh. (1) Go around mesh board. (2) Bring twine up to above knot. (3) Knot over the original knot. (4) Bring working twine down.

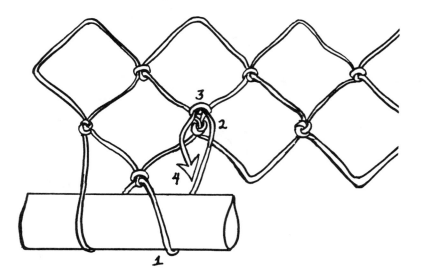

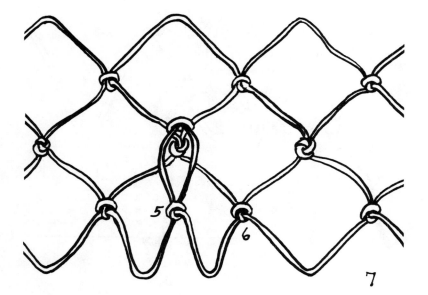

Figure 2-20. Making a false mesh, continued. (5) Knot even with working row. (6) Make next mesh. (7) Continue netting.

7

Sometimes narrowing can be done successfully along the edge of the net. Instead of starting the second row (or the row that one wishes to narrow) by netting the first mesh, omit the first mesh and double the lead twine back on itself, knotting it to the base of the last loop of the preceding row. Then continue to net the row by going into the next or second mesh. This doubling back the twine helps to create a reinforced edge [*figure 2-21*].

A second method is to net two meshes together by putting the needle through two successive loops and tying a weaver's knot around both meshes [*figure 2-22*].

Decreasing by omitting every other mesh at the edges of the net is usually referred to as "fly netting." This gives the

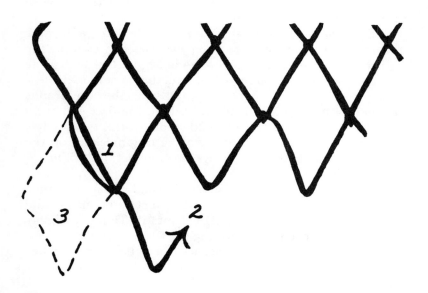

Figure 2-21. Narrowing.
(1) Double down on mesh and knot.
(2) Continue netting into next loop.
(3) Dotted mesh has been omitted.

Figure 2-22. Netting two meshes together.

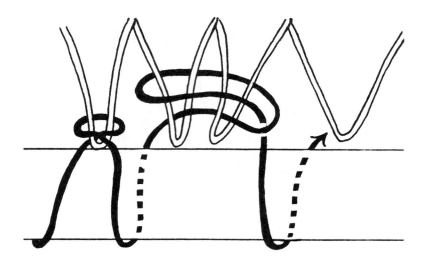

Figure 2-23. Fly netting.

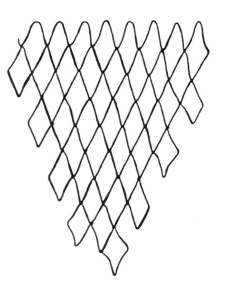

finished net a looped effect. To do this, simply omit netting the last loop of each row. Turn the work and start another row, again omitting the last loop [*figure 2-23*].

Tying on the Twine

When the needle is empty it is rewound and the new length of twine tied to the end left on the net. It is desirable to have this joining knot as inconspicuous as possible and at the same time strong enough that it will not pull out. There are several ways of doing this, but most fishermen join twine with what is called a water knot. Take the end of the new twine and the old piece and lay them together so that they overlap two or three inches. Tie an overhand knot in the end of one piece and thread the end from the other twine through the loop, in the direction of the opposite end. The end should lead away from the knot. Make another overhand knot with the other loose end and the other piece of twine. Pull the twine so that the two knots butt. [*See figure 2-24.*]

Some netters use a fisherman's knot to join two lengths of twine. Start as if you were tying your shoes by crossing the right-hand end over and under the left-hand free end. Take both ends to the top, and taking the end that is now on the left, cross over the original left-hand end. Pinch the two strands together with the other hand and thread the first end down through the lines of the original knot on the inner edge. Take the other end down through the original knot on the outer edge. Pull both sides to tighten the knot. [*See figure 2-25.*]

Another method is to reinforce the end of the new twine with an overhand knot, slacken the last knot made, and (following the lines of the knot) net into it. This is probably the least conspicuous way of tying on.

Occasionally one see instances in which a netter has

simply tied the two ends together with an overhand knot. This is apt to be untidy and the knot is often in the way when making the next mesh with the new twine.

Figure 2-24. Water knot.

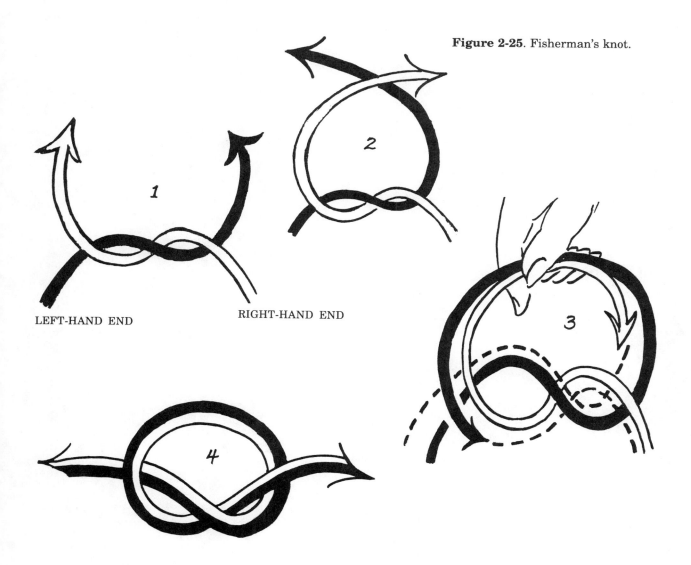

Figure 2-25. Fisherman's knot.

LEFT-HAND END

RIGHT-HAND END

3 Useful Knots for Netting

The following knots are used at various times to attach or join nets or to prevent raveling. These useful knots, plus the rolling hitch (described on p. 83), the weaver's knot or sheet bend (pages 24–30), the water knot (p. 33), and the fisherman's knot (p. 33), form the netmaker's basic repertoire.

Defining a few very general terms might be helpful before I give specific instructions for individual knots. A *bight* is a loop in the twine, or it can be that part of the twine between the end and the standing part. The *lead twine* is the *working end*, which is self-explanatory. The *standing part* is that part of the twine which is not the bight or either end. A *bend* is any method of binding two ends together, such as a "sheet bend." A *hitch* is a method of securing twine to another object, such as a ring, rope, or post—for example, a "clove hitch."

Bowline

Often used to start the first mesh when using the chain start, it has the advantage of not slipping but may be loosened easily when necessary. Start the knot by making a loop over the standing part. Bring the lower end up through the loop. Go behind and around the upper end and back down through the loop. Pull to tighten.

The way Vinalhaven kids learn to make a bowline is by repeating this verse:

A tree had a hole in *front*.
A rabbit popped out of the hole,
Ran around behind the tree,
And jumped back into the hole.

Overhand Knot

Cross one end of twine over another, leaving a loop. Continue drawing this end down behind and up in front of the crossed strand.

Figure 3-1. Bowline.

(1)

(2)

(3)

Figure 3-2. Overhand knot.

Figure 3-3. Multiple overhand knot; double, triple, or overhand bend; or blood knot.

Figure 3-4. Granny knot.

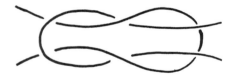

Figure 3-5. Square knot, flat knot, or reef knot.

Multiple Overhand Knot; Double, Triple, or Overhand Bend

Continue the overhand knot further by going down behind and up in front of the crossed strand multiple times. Pull evenly and briskly when tightening.

Blood Knot

Make a multiple overhand knot, crossing twice only. It is used to prevent raveling.

Slip Knot

Make an overhand knot, but instead of pulling the end through, loop it and pull on the loop. (Illustrated on page 40.)

Granny Knot

Although similar to the square knot, this is not as effective. Cross one strand over another, leaving a bight just as in making an overhand knot. Continue drawing this strand end down behind and up in front of the crossed strand. Repeat this process directly above, crossing the second time in the same direction as you did the first time.

Square, or Reef, Knot

This knot is superior to the granny knot, for it pulls more evenly. Start again as if making an overhand knot. Continue as for the granny knot but make your second cross opposite from the first cross. If you put the right-hand strand over in the first cross, use the left-hand strand over in the second cross.

When used in netting, the reef knot is fairly simple to make but does not hold tight. It is used when a flat knot is necessary (indeed, it is often called a flat knot) or for very fine seines where working clearance for the needle is limited, or in instances where the net is to be pulled taut and secured (the tension on the net holds the knots in place).

To make the knot, bring the working twine up behind

Figure 3-6. Netting the reef knot.

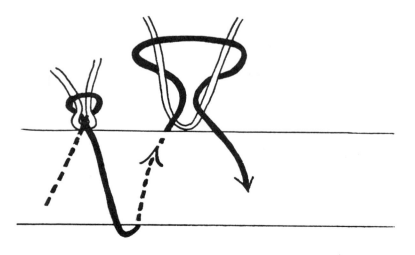

the mesh board and enter the loop of the above row from the front. Pull the twine out to the left rear, coming around in front of the two strands, and reenter the loop from the right rear. Bring the twine forward and pull down to tighten.

Carrick Bend

This is a good joining knot that holds well and ties evenly. Make a loop with one piece of twine. Then take the second piece to be joined and make a loop facing opposite the first. When doing this, put the twine under and then over each strand.

Half Hitch

A hitch is a method of securing twine to a line or rod. The twine is brought up around the line and over or under the other part of the line. It is rarely used alone, for it does not hold unless backed up by another knot or hitch.

Clove Hitch

Two half hitches made in exactly the same way.

Lark's Head or Cow Hitch

Two half hitches made in opposite directions, one hitch under the line and the other over the line.

Ossel Knot and Ossel Hitch

Nets are sometimes hung to a backing rope by means of short pieces of twine called ossels. The ossel knot is used on the backing rope and an ossel hitch is used on the net headrope.

The knot is made by taking the end twine, making two turns over the backing rope and the standing part of the twine and then making a third turn that is carried across the original two and tucked under the standing part.

The ossel hitch is made by bringing the working end behind and under the head rope, next bringing it up behind the standing part, down around in front of the headrope and back up, over itself, and under the first loop.

Figure 3-7. Carrick bend.

Figure 3-8.

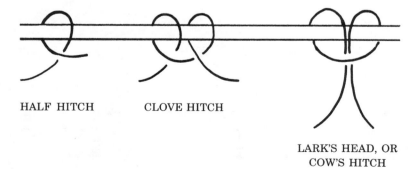

HALF HITCH   CLOVE HITCH

LARK'S HEAD, OR
COW'S HITCH

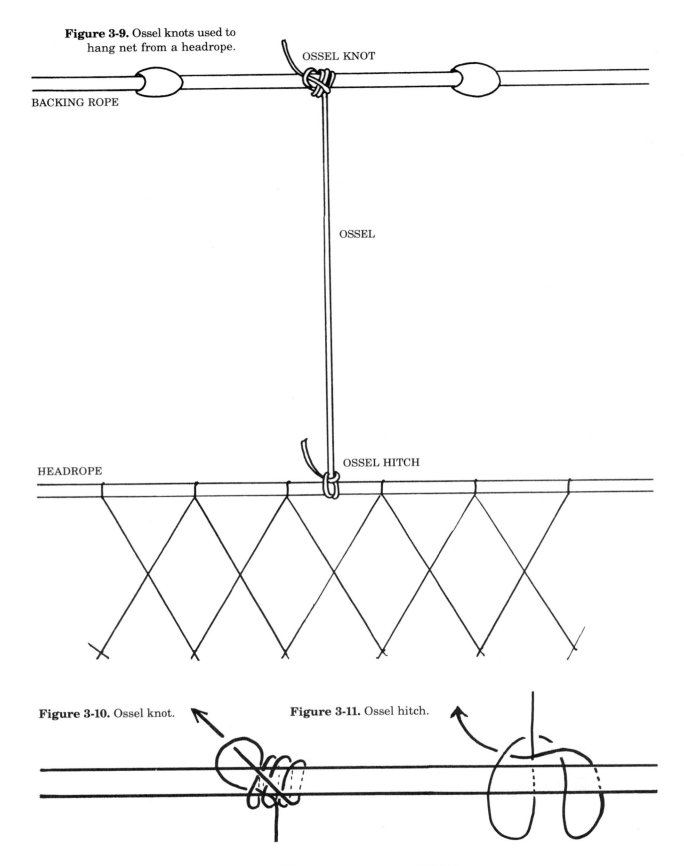

Figure 3-9. Ossel knots used to hang net from a headrope.

OSSEL KNOT

BACKING ROPE

OSSEL

HEADROPE

OSSEL HITCH

Figure 3-10. Ossel knot.

Figure 3-11. Ossel hitch.

4 Circular and Tubular Netting

Round nets are made by netting in a circle. Started at the center and worked toward the outer edge, the circle increases by the addition of meshes. The circle is started either on a grommet or on a foundation loop. If started on a grommet, the meshes are taken up by making the mesh loops in between clove hitches. Enough of a tail end is left to form the last mesh by tying the tail to the working twine. If the circle has a large number of meshes, the hitches stay in place; if fewer are used, the grommet is often bound. The neatest way

Figure 4-1. Clove hitches on grommet. Binding the grommet in between the clove hitches.

39

Figure 4-2. Slip knot.

END TWINE

LEAD
TWINE

to do that is to wrap the twine around the ring, going through each mesh to secure it in position, and tying off by going under the first strands wound.

If the net is started on a foundation loop—as described under Taking Up with a Foundation Loop on pages 21 to 23—the free end of the twine is left long enough to slip through the loop and be pulled tightly after the required number of meshes are cast on, thus forming a circle. Knots made on the foundation loop should be able to *slide*. Check to see that you are making the knots on the foundation loop and not on the lead twine. This is important because you will want to be able to gather the first row of knots together to make a tight circle by pulling on the foundation loop. If the knots are accidentally made on the lead twine instead, they will not pull up correctly. Also, in most cases it is not necessary to tie the working end to a separate foundation loop, for one can simply make the foundation loop on the end of the twine used to make the rest of the net.

After the original meshes are taken up, most circular nets may be hung on a nail and the rows worked around quite easily, but for a large flat circle it is sometimes better to peg the work on a flat surface, physically moving around the work as one nets.

The circular net is augmented by making a series of increases around the perimeter of the work. It is preferable not to make increases under earlier increases, but to enlarge the circle by increasing in alternate rows instead

Figure 4-3. Putting the end twine through the loop.

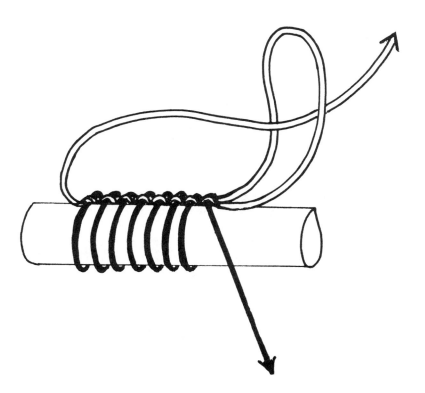

Figure 4-4. Enlarging the circle.
Rows 1, 2, and 3: 8 meshes.
Row 4: increased by 8, to 16.
Row 5: increased by 16, to 32.

[*figure 4-4*]. When the desired circumference is reached, the end is secured by a double weaver's knot.

When making a straight net, one can usually keep as many meshes on the board as is convenient, but on a circular net, the meshes are very apt to be distorted if one continues working meshes and leaving them on the board. Keep moving the board frequently, shifting it into the next meshes to keep the work even and circular. Three to four meshes are all that should be held on the board at any one time.

Tubular or bag-type nets may be fashioned in the same way as a circle. Once the circular base of the bag is wide enough, the tube is formed by netting around the net but not widening any further. The top of the bag can be completed with a drawstring or handle. The thermos bottle cover is made this way.

Sometimes tubular bags are not started in the center but on the outer edge, particularly if it is necessary to put the tube on a rigid holder, as in the case of some minnow nets, butterfly, or basketball nets. In this case, the net is taken up originally on the rigid frame, either by using a chain start and threading the holder through the meshes, or by taking up with clove hitches cast on the holder. (In some instances, one casts on by threading the twine through holes in the frame made especially for that particular net.)

In both circular and tubular nets, the end of each line of rows is attached to the first mesh in the row to complete the circle and yield a round net. One method of doing this (when

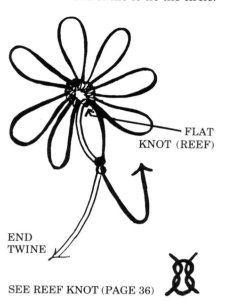

Figure 4-5. Bringing down the end twine to tie the circle.

FLAT KNOT (REEF)

END TWINE

SEE REEF KNOT (PAGE 36)

starting with a foundation loop) is to leave the end of the loop one-third longer than half the diameter of the finished circle. Count the knots on the board, making sure that you have the correct number of knots for the number of meshes needed. (For example, if eight meshes are needed, there should be eight knots on the board, but seven loops around the mesh board below. The last, or eighth, mesh is formed by using the end of the foundation loop and the lead twine.) In reality these meshes will be not full, but half-meshes, which becomes apparent as the work continues.

After the foundation loop is pulled to make the center, it is secured by tying a flat knot (reef knot). The loose end of the foundation loop is pulled down even with the bottom of the row of meshes, and a regular weaver's knot is made with this end and the lead twine. This gives the last mesh for the row. In each succeeding row the foundation loop end is pulled down and the connecting mesh made. [*Figure 4-5.*]

Another method used to connect the rows is called *dropping down* [*figure 4-6*]. The first row is knotted together at the top and the working end is brought down to the bottom of the last mesh and a weaver's knot made. The next row is netted. Then the working end is brought down around the mesh board, making a connecting mesh (a), brought up through the next above strands, and a weaver's knot made over the knot formed when the first drop was made (b). The twine is brought down and knotted to the bottom of the lower mesh at (c) and the next row (d) netted. Again the twine is brought around the mesh board and the process repeated on subsequent rows until the desired length is reached. The disadvantage of this method is that it creates a double line of twine running diagonally down one side of the net.

In some cases, particularly on bait bags, bringing the row down evenly is not necessary, and one simply continues on to the next row in a spiral fashion. This leaves an uneven edge on the finished product, for the last row is left on the outer circle and the endpoint will be obvious. (See Bait Bag pattern.)

Many bags are made by not netting in a circle at all but by making a rectangular net the width and length of the bag and then netting it together at two edges. The Glass Float Cover pattern described below is a practice piece for this method. The bottom of the rectangular piece is pulled together and knotted, then the piece is turned, put on a hook, and the sides knotted together, making an added mesh.

The Laundry Bag pattern (in the Projects chapter) is made in the same fashion and has a drawstring closure at the top.

The Shopping Bag pattern, as well as the forge-welded Scallop Drag, are started by netting a square or rectangle as a base, increasing at the corners to make the base somewhat circular, and then netting a tube to complete the bag. Using the same square base, one can decrease at the corners to produce a large base with a tubular slanting top.

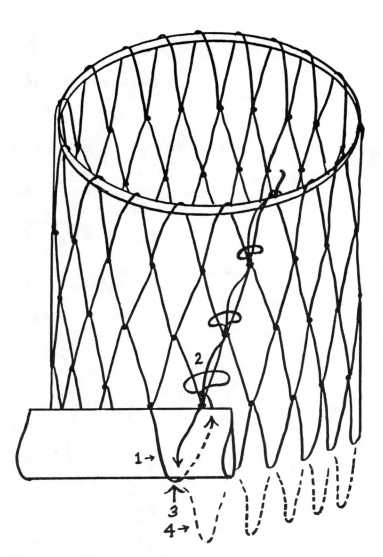

Figure 4-6. Dropping down. (1) Connecting mesh; (2) upper knot through upper strands; (3) position for dropped knot; (4) new row.

Four Practice Pieces

GLASS FLOAT COVER

Although the colorful glass floats blown in the glass houses of Germany and Austria are now antiques, some people still come across one that has been forgotten in a corner of an old fish shack or attic and want to hang it in a net cover for decoration. This is a good practice piece illustrating one way of tying a net to form a bag (making a tube from a flat piece). This particular pattern comes from the Ames family on Matinicus. Isabel Osgood got three cents apiece making them for her father, old Vonnie Ames, when she was in grammar school.

Glass float covers.
Charlotte Goodhue photo.

Use nylon twine #36 or nylon heading twine #550 and a ³/₄-inch mesh board, and work with the old-fashioned netting method (page 24).

1. Take up 6 meshes (12 knots down) with a chain start (pages 19–21).

2. Put on a stirrup (page 20, steps 6 and 7).

3. Net 6 rows.

4. When at the bottom, put the needle through all of the bottom meshes and secure by going back under the lead twine. Pull tight. Repeat. [*Figure 4-7.*]

5. Take the work off the hook. Remove the stirrup. Reverse the work, hanging the bottom on the hook.

6. Find the first row of knots and knot the lead twine to the middle of the mesh on the other side even with the row [*(a) on figure 4-8*].

7. Drop down and repeat even with the next row of knots (b). Repeat at points (c), (d), and (e). This will give 7 meshes on the finished bag instead of the original 6.

8. Put a drawstring on the free edge. Fit onto the glass float and tie. [*Figure 4-9.*]

Figure 4-7. Gathering the bottom meshes.

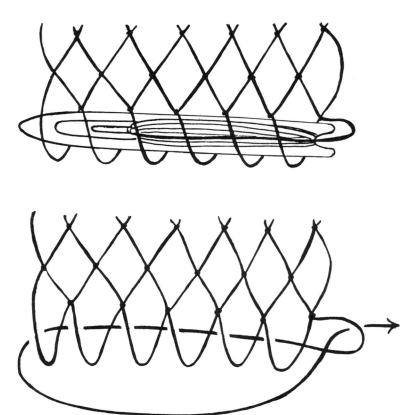

Figure 4-8. Knotting the edges together to form a tube.

Figure 4-9. Completed float cover.

THERMOS BOTTLE COVER

We originally made thermos bottle covers from stout twine with small meshes, the heavy twine with its thick knots acting as a buffer to prevent breakage. After stainless steel thermos bottles appeared on the market, breakage was no longer a problem, but what a nuisance to grab a bare thermos and get aboard a boat when one's arms are usually loaded with other necessities for the trip! The thermos cover, with its long string handles, makes it possible to sling it over one's arm and get going or to hang it on a nail out of the way.

This pattern illustrates how to start a circle on a foundation loop. In this case, the circle is not increased beyond a certain point, so that instead of lying flat the netting becomes a tube. The side of the tube is joined by netting the rows together with a tail from the foundation loop and the lead twine.

Use #550 nylon twine and 1-inch and 2¹/₂-inch mesh boards. Work in the new-fashioned netting method (page 27).

1. Make a foundation loop with a slip knot that will slide on an 18-inch tail. (See page 36.)

2. Working across one side of the foundation loop, take up 11 meshes on the 2¹/₂-inch board. Put the tail through the

Thermos bottle cover.
Charlotte Goodhue photo.

foundation loop and pull tightly so that the loop disappears and a grommet is formed. Secure with a reef knot.

3. Make the twelfth mesh by tying the tail of the foundation loop and the lead twine with a weaver's knot, keeping the knot level with the base of the meshes already made. This gives an added mesh, making 12 meshes instead of 11 in each row.

4. Net the next row. At the end of the row, knot the foundation and the lead twine again with a netting knot, keeping the knot level with the row of knots just formed.

5. Net down in this fashion for 9 more rows, then change to the smaller mesh board. Net the last row on the 1-inch mesh board and tie the lead twine and the loop end with a weaver's knot.

6. Continue using the smaller mesh board as you work the handle, as that will give it greater strength. Start the handle as if you were beginning another row by netting into the next two meshes. Net the two meshes down for 36 rows.

7. Hold this length out straight to be sure that there are no twists and net into two meshes on the main piece, forming the handle. To do this evenly, skip one mesh to the right of the beginning of the handle and net into the next two meshes.

8. Tie off the cord by making a small overhand knot close to the last knot made. Cut the twine (and if it is nylon, melt it).

9. Skip the next mesh, make a small overhand knot in the end of the lead twine and net into the next two meshes. Net the second handle down for 36 meshes. Skip one mesh at the top of the bag and net the handle into the next two meshes. Secure with an overhand knot in the lead twine. Cut (and if needed, melt the end of) the twine.

BAIT BAGS

Everyone makes bait bags differently. Some bags are made much like the Glass Float Cover by netting a straight piece, tying the end, and then netting it together. The following pattern is one of the quickest, for it incorporates the foundation loop as a later drawstring, and is the way the older netters on Vinalhaven's Calderwood Neck did theirs. This net is worked in a spiral, and, since the meshes are small, it is made with the new-fashioned netting technique (page 27).

Use string or nylon twine #36, a 1-inch mesh board, and a needle slightly less than 1/2-inch wide. (If you use a long needle, you will not have to reload before finishing a bag.)

1. Tie together the ends of a 2-foot length of twine.

2. Make an overhand knot in the doubled twine about one third of the way from one end, leaving a loop on the doubled end.

3. Use this as a foundation loop and tie on the lead twine. [*Figure 4-10.*]

4. Take up 14 meshes, but instead of knotting the first

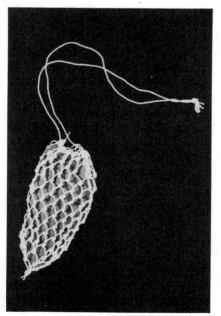

Bait Bag. Charlotte Goodhue photo.

Figure 4-10. Foundation loop for bait bag.

meshes on top of the mesh board, as is usually done when taking up on a foundation loop, drop down the length of a mesh and knot below. This gives a row of top meshes with no knots [*see figure 4-11*] and a first row of meshes that are an even size. The twine is still going up through the foundation loop, but the knot is being made below instead of on the loop. Keep the strain even while dropping the knots.

5. Connect the row by netting right into the first mesh. There will be a small distortion, but this will not be noticed when the bag is finished. Continue to net the rows, going into the first mesh of each row and making a spiral effect.

6. Net down 9 rows.

7. Narrow on the tenth row by netting every 2 meshes together.

8. Put the needle through the remaining 7 meshes, pull tightly together, and tie off with 2 slip knots.

9. Cut the twine.

10. Turn the bag to the top, remove the overhand knot that was made on the length of twine, and the bag opens with the drawstring already on it.

A third method of making a bait bag is to proceed as just described but do not narrow on the tenth row. Instead, end the

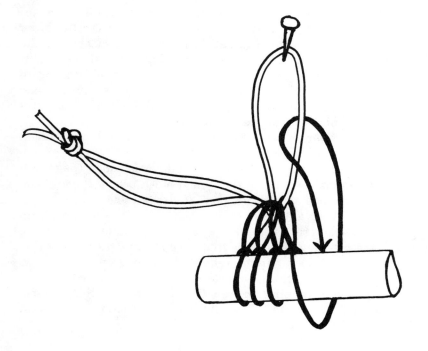

Figure 4-11. Knotting below the mesh board for the first row.

netting by making a double sheet bend in the last mesh and cut off the twine. The side with the foundation loop is the bottom of the bag. Tie the loop tightly and cut the twine. The tenth, or last, row is the top of the bag and needs a drawstring threaded through the meshes to complete it.

SHOPPING BAG #1

This particular pattern has been popular for many years on Vinalhaven and is similar to the shopping bags seen throughout Europe. In the past, bags were netted from off-white cotton, which lent a seacoast charm and an almost homespun quality, but nowadays the bags are made from brightly colored or shiny white nylon. The bags are gay, the colors vibrant.

The Shopping Bag can be worked with either the old-fashioned or new-fashioned netting method (pages 24 to 30). The technique for making the bag is somewhat different from other tubular or circular nets in that the netting begins with a square or rectangle as the base. The base is increased (widened) at the corners, which converts it to a more circular shape. It is then netted in a spiral fashion until the top is reached. The top is pulled in by netting the last two rows on a smaller mesh board, and a reinforced edge added by working the last row with double twine.

There are several ways of finishing the top. The most common is to crochet into each mesh along the edge: single crochet for a small opening, two single crochet stitches for a medium opening, or three single crochet stitches for a larger opening. Use a size E crochet hook.

The top is then divided into fourths. The two handles are attached on two opposite fourths and are made from a single-crocheted chain that is attached and then reinforced and broadened by crocheting back over the chain with another row of single crochet. People who do not crochet often finish the bag by making half-hitches on the meshes at the top and form the handles by alternating left and right half-hitches across two lenghts of attached twine, similar to macramé. A third method is to net the handles onto the bag as shown in Shopping Bag #2, which follows, and still another technique is to insert a drawstring.

Use nylon twine #18 and 2-inch and 1-inch mesh boards.

1. Take up 17 meshes on a foundation loop (page 21). Net down six rows using the 2-inch mesh board. Remove the foundation loop and lay the piece flat on a table.

2. Taking a piece of twine about 18 inches long, pick up the meshes across the middle of the rectangle, leaving the outside mesh on both sides free. [*See figure 4-12.*] Using this piece of twine as a stirrup, rehang the work from a nail.

3. Net into the first side mesh and widen one in this mesh (see Widening, page 30). Net around the square, widening one in each first mesh on each side. You should end up with 21 meshes.

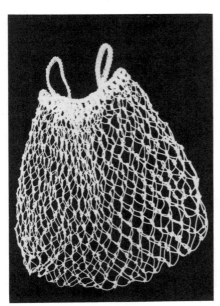

Shopping bag with crocheted handles. Charlotte Goodhue photo.

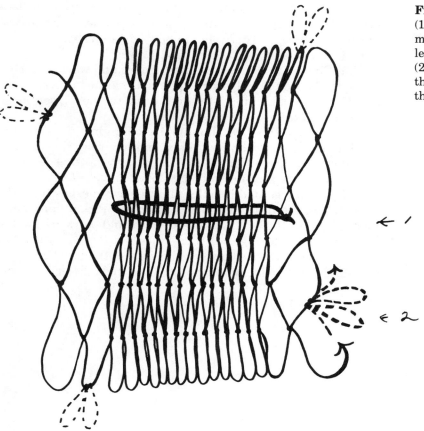

Figure 4-12.
(1) Pick up the middle row of meshes with a length of twine, leaving the outside meshes free. (2) On the first row netted around the square, widen one mesh in the first mesh on each side.

4. Net the 21 meshes in spiral fashion for 14 rows. (This may be increased for a larger bag.)

5. Change to the 1-inch mesh board and net the next row on the smaller board.

6. Change to double twine on the needle and work the last row on the smaller mesh board using double twine.

7. Knot the end twine. (If using nylon, melt the frayed ends with a lighted match.) Finish the handles using any of the methods described above.

SHOPPING BAG #2 (WITH NETTED HANDLES)

Use nylon twine #18 and 1¼-inch and ½-inch mesh boards.

1. Take up 40 meshes on a foundation loop (page 21) using the larger mesh board. Net down 11 rows, working with either the old-fashioned or new-fashioned netting method (pages 24 to 30). Remove the foundation loop and lay the piece flat on a table.

2. Pick up the meshes across the middle of the piece with an 18-inch length of twine, leaving the outside meshes free on each side. [*See figure 4-12 above.*] Using this piece of twine as a stirrup, hang the work from a nail.

Shopping bag with netted handles. Charlotte Goodhue photo.

3. Net into the first side mesh and widen one in this mesh. Net around the square, widening one in each first mesh on each side. There should now be 44 meshes.

4. Net in a spiral fashion for 16 rows.

5. Change to the 1/2-inch mesh board and work 4 meshes to begin the handle. (This line of small meshes prevents the handle from stretching.) Change back to the larger mesh board and net these four meshes down 12 rows.

6. Finish the first handle by changing back to the smaller mesh board and working another row, then attach the handle to the other side of the bag by netting it into 4 meshes with the pick-up stitch described on page 59.

7. For the second handle, count over 8 meshes from the point where the first handle was attached. Pick up and net 4 meshes using the 1/2-inch mesh board and work as for the first handle, attaching the other end to 4 meshes on the other side, leaving 8 meshes between the ends of the handle.

8. Cut the twine, knot the end (and melt the end if using nylon).

5 Square Netting, Reverse Netting, and Selvedges

Square Netting

Square netting is used when a rigid net is required. Because the sides of the mesh are parallel to each other, the net holds its shape. Quite the opposite is true of the diamond mesh, where rigidity is obtained by stretching the net lengthwise, or "with the run," and securing it with a stout line or pipe—or, as in the case of a lobster trap head, with funny eyes (metal hoops), lacing, or nailing. But if a net needs to be in place by its own merit—the most obvious examples are tennis and badminton nets—square meshes are essential. The square mesh not only keeps its shape but has the added advantage of a reinforced edge, making its own selvedge as the twine is brought down to form the rows. In cases where added reinforcement is needed, the outside edge may be caught in when the last mesh is made in each row.

Start a square netting project by tying the twine onto a stirrup (which will later be removed) and taking up two meshes. Turn the work, net into these two meshes and increase by adding one false mesh (as described in Widening, p. 30) in the last mesh. Turn the work and net into these three meshes, widening again in the last mesh by making another false mesh. Continue widening in each row until desired length is reached. As you progress, you will note that the mesh is being worked diagonally, and the first mesh made is in the upper left-hand corner. At this point, there will be two more meshes on the board than on the left-hand side. For example, if the side of the square has eight meshes there would be ten on the board.

To turn the corner—and this will be the lower left hand corner of your net—decrease one mesh by narrowing at the end of the row. This decrease forms a right angle. Continue to decrease one mesh in every row until there are two left. Do not net these, but instead pull them together and knot them securely. Untie the stirrup in the opposite corner and finish

Figure 5-1. Square netting.

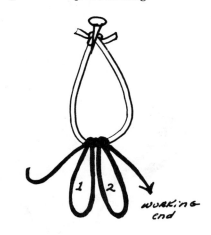

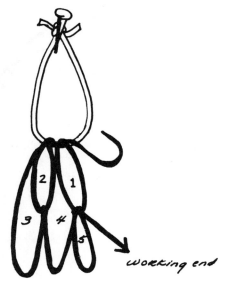

51

Figure 5-2.

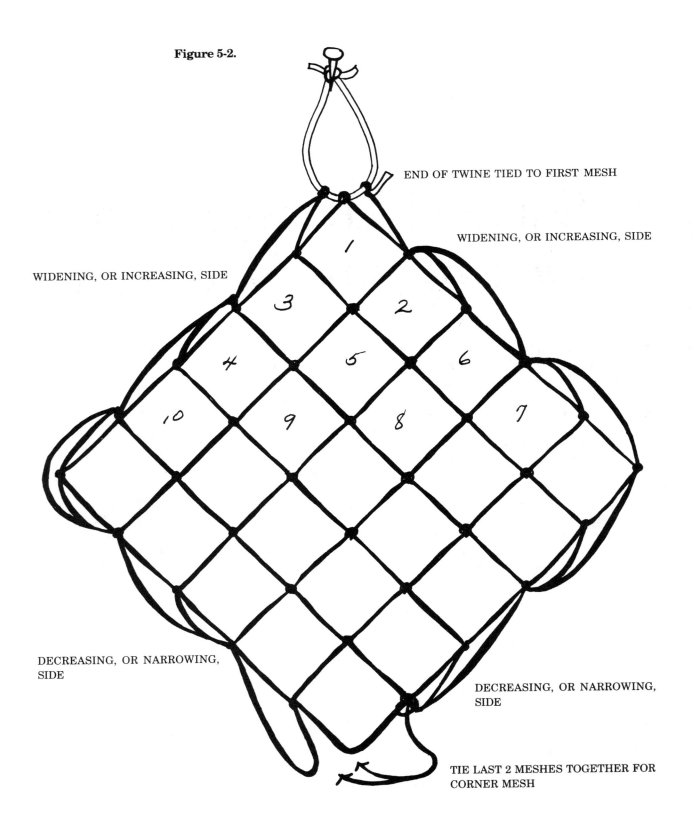

END OF TWINE TIED TO FIRST MESH

WIDENING, OR INCREASING, SIDE

WIDENING, OR INCREASING, SIDE

1

3 2

4 5 6

10 9 8 7

DECREASING, OR NARROWING, SIDE

DECREASING, OR NARROWING, SIDE

TIE LAST 2 MESHES TOGETHER FOR CORNER MESH

off the first mesh in the same way by tying the end. The resulting net will be a square, with all four sides equal.

To make a rectangular net with square meshes, follow the directions for the square, but when the lower left-hand corner is reached and the corner turned at a right angle by decreasing the last mesh, work across the breadth of the rectangle by increasing at the end of the next row and decreasing on the following row. Continue alternately increasing and decreasing until reaching the desired breadth. Stop at the upper right-hand corner. At this point, there should again be two more meshes than is required for the depth of the rectangle. The upper right corner, the right side, and the base are finished by decreasing at the end of every row until two meshes remain. Tie these together to form one mesh, as described in instructions for the square.

Reverse Netting

Most netting is done from left to right. At the end of each row the work is turned over so that the next row is again worked from left to right. Turning the work is not always possible, however, particularly if it is on a rigid holder. If space is limited, one cannot always solve the problem by moving behind the work to the other side. If one continues to work from left to right without turning the work over completely, a twist will appear in the finished piece. The most feasible method of avoiding twisting is to net in reverse, that is net from right to left. This is not difficult, and with a few practice meshes, one can master the technique easily.

There are two methods of reverse netting. The first is essentially the same as netting from left to right except that the twine is pulled down *behind* and up in *front* of the board to enter the preceding mesh *from front to back*. Then the same swing is used to leave a loop (as on the knot made from left to right), the needle is put under the two strands from the preceding mesh (as in the usual weaver's knots), in front of the twine made by the arc, and the knot is pulled tight. [*See Figure 5-3.*]

The second method needs more dexterity. This is to actually make the entire knot in reverse. Bring the twine under the mesh board from the front, up the back, and enter the preceding mesh from the back. Pulling forward, make the arc by going to the left, but in this instance go behind the two strands of the loop of the preceding mesh. Cross over the strands in front, under the arc formed, and pull the knot tight. [*See figure 5-4.*]

Selvedges

Square netting makes its own selvedge, for as the square is netted the twine brought down from the preceeding row helps reinforce the edge. This does not normally happen when one is netting a diamond shape, for in that case the edge is serrated, yet many diamond-meshed pieces do need a selvedge. In cases where it is not necessary to make a

Figure 5-3. Reverse netting, first method.

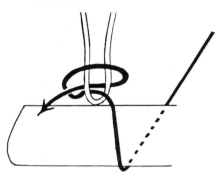

Figure 5-4. Reverse netting, second method.

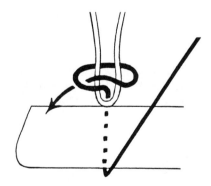

Figure 5-5. Taking in the descending twine on the first mesh made in each row.

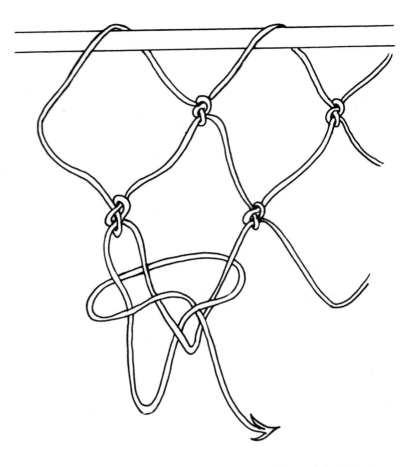

selvedge at the top or bottom because the net will later be mounted or put on a rod, the side edges may be reinforced by taking in the descending outside twine and the left side of the upper mesh as if they were one strand. [*Figure 5-5.*]

The only drawback to this method is that the selvedge on the first row will not be drawn in but must be tied in when the net is completed—and one must not forget that the width of the net is now reduced by one mesh.

Selvedges along the bottom or top of the net may be made quite easily by netting the first and last rows with double twine (see Winding the Needle, page 9).

Figure 5-6. Double selvedge on bottom of net. Last row is netted with a double-threaded needle.

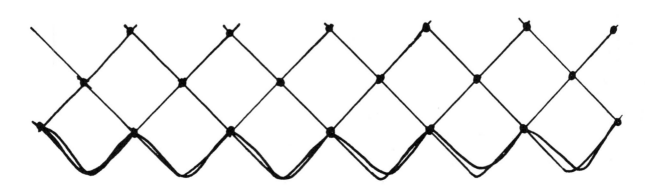

6 Mending, Patching, and Lacing

Mending

Frequently fishing nets rip, and repairs often must be made on crowded decks, where the cold wind and buffeting waves hamper the mending. If the repairs cannot be done on the spot, the boat must return to shore and the catch must be postponed. An understanding of net repair is essential for those fishermen who are seining, gill netting, or trawling, and often the repairs must be done speedily. An experienced fisherman tells the story of a mender who did perfect work but was very slow. As the hours passed, the upset crew had to keep reminding him that there were no fish on the deck!

Today, the larger nets used for dragging are machine made, some knotted, braided, or even interwoven, but the

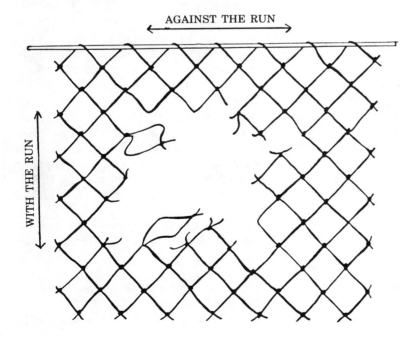

AGAINST THE RUN

WITH THE RUN

Figure 6-1. Portion of damaged net hung "with the run."

55

basic design is the same when made into the fishing net. The pull of the intersecting diamond is in the same direction. The depth goes "with the run," adding strength to the net, while the width is "against the run." In other words, the depth of the net is what takes the stress, and the netted knots will tighten when pulled down, or with the depth. Going against the run is to pull sideways on the net, which may loosen the knots. A net must be properly positioned to be mended correctly and placed so that the netter works across the rows, filling in the missing gaps and netting down to the next row in the manner the net was originally put into the seine or trawl. If in doubt, cut away a mesh. If it is hung correctly, a loop will remain intact in the above mesh; if incorrect, the mesh will open.

The net may be hung to facilitate mending in a variety of ways. If the net is large and heavy and the hole small, it is often bunched up so that the hole is forward and the bunch lashed to a post, or it can be strung so that a rope holds the damaged section upright. (A friend of ours holds open rips with his toes.) The important principle is to follow the lay of the twine so that the point of the elongated diamond hangs down.

After the net is positioned, the damaged part is cut away. As already mentioned, the loops along the upper and lower edges remain intact even after the broken strands are removed. These are known as "clean" meshes; conversely, the side meshes open up when knots are removed and are known as "cut," or "broken," meshes. Ragged side ends (and knots often left in the top and bottom meshes, to save time) are, whenever possible, cut half an inch from the adjacent knot to prevent raveling. The cutting is done usually with an ordinary pocket knife, put under the strands and turned toward the mender as the cut is made (called "snapping out"). For good mending, all meshes should be clean on the top and the knots left in along the sides.

In an undamaged net, all of the knots have four strands, but once the net is torn, the number of strands left on the remaining knots varies. The crux of proper mending, in order to finish with the netting correct, is to start the mending at the top of the rip on a three-legger and end at the bottom on a three-legger. (A "three-legger" is a knot with three strands coming from it.) All other meshes picked up must be cut away so that only two or four strands are left leading from the knot. If, when cutting the damaged area, a three-legger is found, the bottom strand facing the hole must be cut away.

The knots described are given in the order used to mend the net in Figure 6-2, beginning with the starter knot.

The Starter Knot

Starting at the top left-hand side on a three-legger, leave an inch of slack in the end of the twine.

(When some netting is begun, as in the chain start, it is

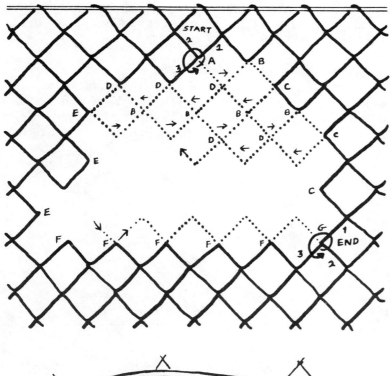

Figure 6-2. Always start and end with a three-legger. All other meshes left are two- or four-leggers. In this example, the mending knots are worked in this order:
A. Starter knot
B. Half mesh knot from left to right.
C. Sider knot made on the right.
D. Half mesh knot from right to left.
E. Sider knot made on the left.
Continue as established until last row.
F. Pick up knots along lower edge.
G. Finishing knot.

Figure 6-3. Starter knot.

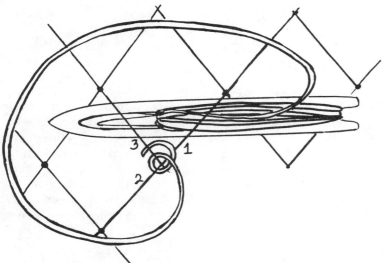

customary to put a small overhand knot in the end of the twine to secure the first netting knot. This is not done in mending, for the added knot adds bulk and may catch on other meshes when the net is fished or thrown overboard.)

Go behind and under strands 3 and 2 (as shown in *figure 6-3*), coming up in the mesh over strand 1, swing to the left and make a weavers' knot, holding the inch of slack so that it will not pull through. Do not tighten, but swing to the left again and make a second weaver's knot directly into the first. Now tighten both.

Another variation of the starter knot is to make the weaver's knot and tighten it, then swing as if to make another, but instead go under one strand only, which makes an added hitch. This method has the advantage of making a less bulky knot.

Half-Mesh Knot from Left to Right

Net in the regular fashion, picking up the clean meshes from left to right, making the weaver's knot and leaving half-meshes between each knot to match the net. Most menders omit the board and use their fingers to gauge the size of the mesh.

Figure 6-4. Half mesh knot from left to right (regular netting).

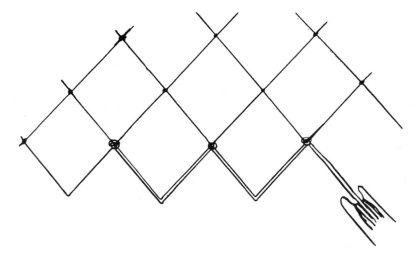

Sider Knot Made on the Right

Bring the twine down from the upper mesh in proportion with the bar measurment and place the twine just to the right of the side knot. Hold it there with your thumb and forefinger just beneath and behind the knot. Go under the upper strand of the side knot and the new strand formed by the mending twine. Pull tight. Make an arc and go under both strands, then over the loop, and pull down tight. The second hitch is sometimes omitted by some menders, particularly on fine mesh such as herring gear.

Half-Mesh Knot from Right to Left

This is the same as reverse netting. If the net is large, it cannot be turned to work from the other side continuing from left to right. Consequently, the netter works back across the row by reversing the knot. The twine is pulled down from behind and up in front of the mesh board or fingers, entering the above mesh from front to back, or going "down through." Then the same swing is used to leave the arc, the needle is shuttled under the two strands and in front of the twine made by the arc.

Sider Knot Made on the Left

This is simply the reverse of the sider knot made on the right. Pull the twine down just to the left of the side knot,

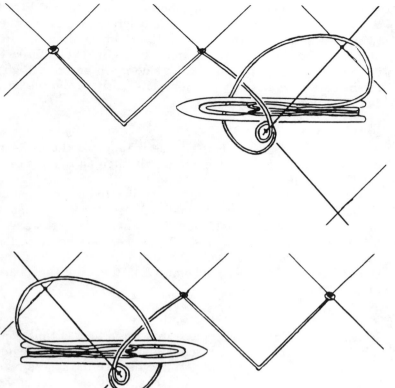

Figure 6-5. Sider knot made on the right.

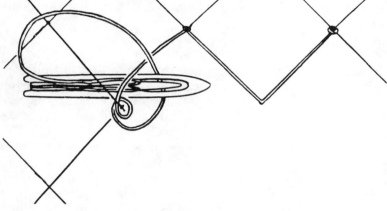

Figure 6-6. Sider knot made on the left.

allowing for proper length of the bar, and hold tightly between the forefinger and thumb. Go under the upper strand of the side knot and the new strand formed by the mending twine. Pull tight. Make an arc and go under both strands, then over the loop, and pull down tight. The second hitch is sometimes omitted by some menders, particularly on fine mesh such as herring gear.

Pick-Up Knots

When the bottom of the hole is reached, the intact lower meshes must be picked up to make the net continuous. If the pick-up falls so that it is worked from left to right, come down under and pick up the loop from the left, adjusting the bar measurement to correspond with the mesh size. Pinch the two strands together with the thumb and forefinger. Swing the twine down to the left, making the arc to the right underneath the strands, and enter from right to left under the strands and over the arc. Pull to tighten, making sure the knot falls on the two strands. Actually it is still the weaver's knot, but made upside down.

    If the pick-up falls from right to left, go down under the

MENDING, PATCHING, AND LACING   **59**

Figure 6-7. Pick up knots.

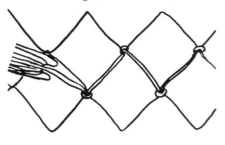

Figure 6-8. Finishing knot.

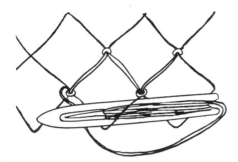

loop from the right, regulating the bar measurement. Pinch the two strands with the thumb and forefinger, swing the twine to the left and then toward the right, making the arc and go under the two strands from the right. The difference in the left or right pick-up is the side mesh entered. Right meshes are entered from the right, left meshes from the left. The knot is made the same.

Finishing Knot

Make a weaver's knot in the same manner as the pick-up knot, but reinforce it by making a half-hitch on the opposite bar from the last bar formed.

Some variations in mending are dictated by the type of twine from which the net is made. A heavy net, such as a drag net, may need a half-hitch on either side of the sheet bend for extra strength, while fine nets—herring gear, for example—are often mended with just a half-hitch along the sides of the rip, the sheet bend omitted, so that bulky knots are at a minimum.

Patching

Netting an entire missing piece in a large tear is time consuming. To avoid this a piece of "slugging twine," a commercially prepared piece of net may be inserted in the hole and attached to the main body of the net. The mesh size of the net and the slugging twine should correspond.

Lay out the net, expose the damaged section, and cut it out. It is not necessary to leave a three-legger at top and bottom as in mending. If the tear is very large, the mending can start by cutting part of the hole, then later cutting more as one works along. Count the meshes across the top of the tear and lay in a piece of slugging twine of the desired size; that is, cut so that it is one mesh smaller than the opening it is to fill. This accommodates the half or quarter mesh that connects the two. For example, if you had a five-mesh opening, the patch should be four meshes.

It is easier to begin at the top left and net either across and down to end in the right-hand corner, or begin at the top right and net down to end in the left hand corner. Then net the opposite section. (If one works all around the net, one set of knots will be pulling in the wrong direction. If, to avoid this, one nets uphill, meshes are apt to be missed.) End by putting a half-hitch on both sides of the last knot.

Lacing

In a rush, fishermen will sometimes lace a net as a temporary measure. The twine is shuttled through the meshes of both sides of the rip and caught together at intervals, usually every six to eight inches. The securing knot is tied only on one side of the tear and is formed by making a half-hitch over and another under an existing knot on a torn side. The lacing is usually removed and replaced by proper mending or patching when time permits.

7 Fishermen's Nets

Lobstering: Trap Heads and Ends

Most people Down East will not hesitate to state that lobster is one of the finest culinary delicacies found anywhere on earth! *Homarus americanus,* usually pictured as a cooked red-orange, is actually dark greenish-blue with green-black mottling. Its native habitat lies along a broad strip of coastal waters from Delaware to the Maritime Provinces.

Square four-header traps with netting on the outside. Charlotte Goodhue photo.

Half-round lobster traps
with netted sides and ends.
Charlotte Goodhue photo.

This crustacean frequents both the relatively shallow waters near the shoreline and the deep waters of the continental shelf. Its ability to live so close to the shore and yet function as well under many fathoms of ocean prompts some people to think that there are two types, the inshore and the offshore lobster. No proof exists for this theory, and even the question of the lobster migrating from inshore to offshore waters has not been fully explored.

The bulk of the American lobster population is off Maine and Nova Scotia. Although the industry first started in Massachusetts in the eighteenth century (a large lobster selling for three half-pence on the Boston market in 1740), a declining catch over the years has resulted in only a handful of lobster fishermen below Kittery.

The scavenging lobster's strong sense of smell attracts it to the baited trap, the bait usually being unmarketable fish, waste trimmings from canneries, fish racks from which fillets have been removed, or oily bait such as pogies or herring. Large bait is strung on a bait line, but when small pieces such as cannery trimmings are used, the bait is

Looking down through the door at the trap's side heads. Charlotte Goodhue photo.

placed in a netted sack called a bait bag. These bags are usually homemade either by the lobsterman or his family. In the past, the material was sisal, manila, or cotton treated to withstand rot. Most bags today are made from synthetic twine, which withstands the stress of seas and weather for long periods without added treatment.

The original method of catching a lobster was with a hoop-net. A net bag about eighteen inches deep was attached to a large 36-inch iron ring; a cord for raising and lowering the ring and the bait was suspended in the center. This method required constant attention, and as lobstering became a profitable industry it was soon replaced by the trap. Although lobsters are also harvested by dragging in deeper offshore waters, it is the classic wood-and-mesh lobster trap, or pot, that people usually associate with Maine's most famous fishery. In the past, traps were made of wood, and the heads, which guide the lobster's entrance, were netted. Today, newer versions and materials (wire and plastic) have appeared, and in many cases the amount of netting in each trap has increased. Replacing wooden laths with lighter netted twine reduces both the trap's weight and buoyancy considerably. End laths may be replaced by netted ends, and in some instances the entire outside body of the trap is netted, leaving only the wooden frame. In the latter case, the netting is usually a net piece purchased for this purpose or cut from discarded pieces of seine net.

Traps may be rectangular in cross-section, called "square" pots, or semi-cylindrical ("half-round"). They are of three general types: the double-header, the parlor trap, and the two-header four-bow trap. The number and arrangement of the netted heads that funnel the catch into the pot vary according to the type of trap. The wider end of the head is nailed or laced to the appropriate opening and the inner end lashed to metal hoops ("funny eyes") that hold the net open and rigid. Brace lines draw the net tight.

Wire traps showing the netted heads inside. Charlotte Goodhue photo.

Lobster heads are all made from the same general pattern, but they vary in size and number of meshes according to individual preference. The patterns offered here are ones that have been used successfully by the lobstermen in my family.

LARGE LOBSTER HEAD

(This head is used for the parlor section of a parlor trap or for both sections in a double header.)

The pattern is "10 and 10, 3 and 10." (This means netting 10 meshes across for 10 rows and then continuing with three meshes across for ten more rows.)

Use a $2^{1/2}$-inch mesh board and #750 nylon twine or heading twine. Work in the old-fashioned method (page 24).

Although many methods of taking up may be used, this pattern calls for the chain start.

1. Tie an overhand knot in the end of the twine. This anchors the first netting knot.

2. Make the first mesh by going around the mesh board twice and making a netting knot over the slip knot. As you make more heads, it will become easier to estimate the size of the first mesh by eye, but for beginners wrapping the twine twice around the mesh board is a reliable way to assure correct size.

3. Turn the mesh so that the netting knot is in the middle of the left side and hang it on a hook.

4. Bring the twine down around the mesh board and up through the first mesh. Be sure to hold the board just below the base of the upper mesh.

5. Continue netting the chain until there are twenty knots.

6. Take up by picking up the meshes on the left side only. (See Taking up With the Chain Start, page 21). Check the protruding meshes to make sure there is the correct number of 10.

7. Put the meshes on a stirrup (see page 20, steps 6 and 7) and hang the stirrup on a hook.

8. Net down until there are ten rows of knots, working across all the meshes.

9. Next net only three meshes across for ten rows more.

10. The long, narrow section must now be netted into the broad upper section. Be sure that the narrow portion does not get twisted in the process. First, bring the lead twine up and into the upper mesh [labeled 1b in figure 7-1]. When doing this, you must allow enough space for the row of connecting meshes to be the same size as the rest of the meshes, so leave enough length in the lead twine to equal two rows of knots. Once you have drawn out enough twine, make a weaver's knot in the end mesh (1b). Now pick up mesh 1a and make a knot, 2b and knot, 2a and knot, 3b and knot, 3a and knot. Tie an overhand knot in the end of the twine close to the last weaver's knot and cut the twine.

(Note: When netting into meshes 1b, 2b, and 3b, you

Figure 7-1. Netting trap heads.

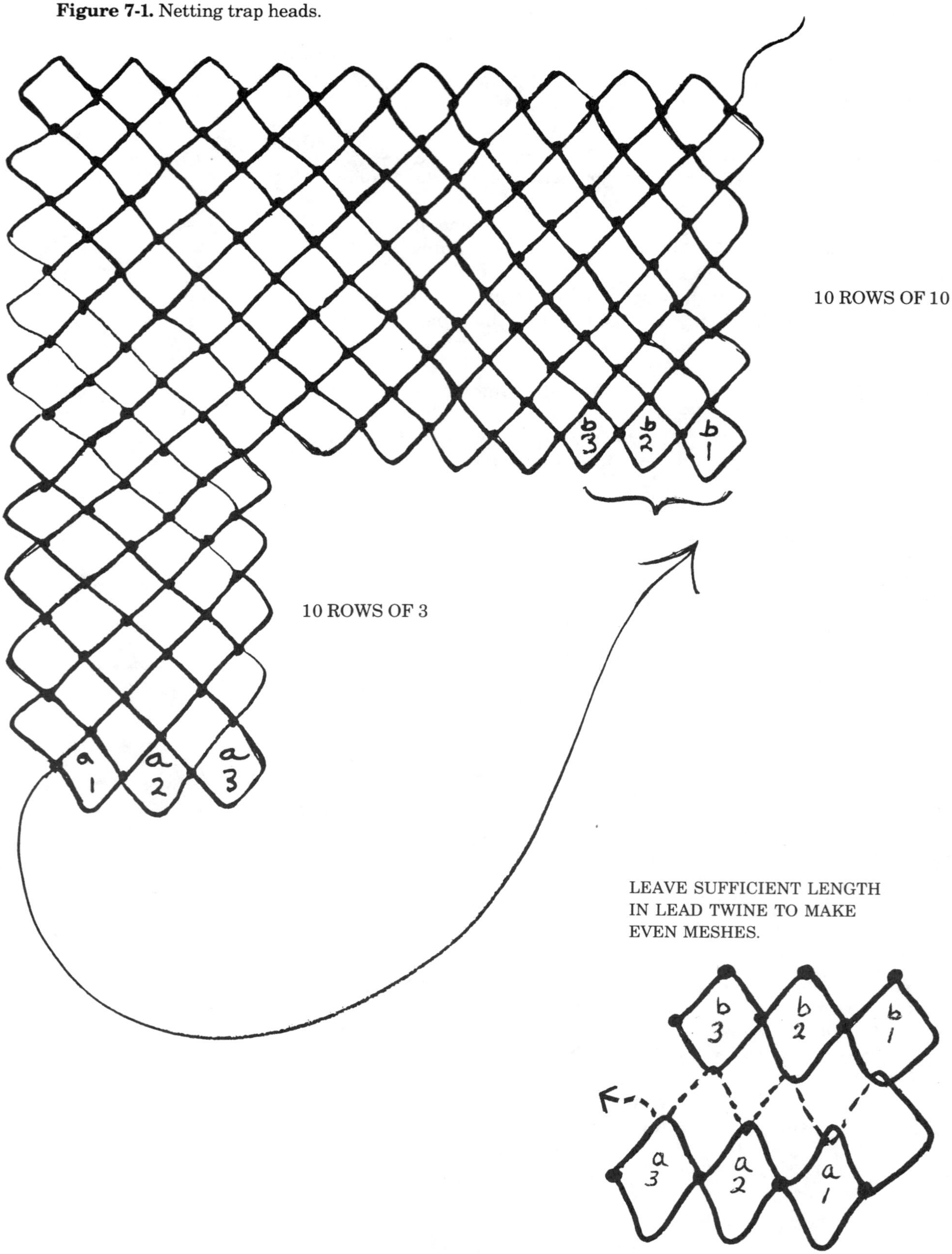
10 ROWS OF 10
10 ROWS OF 3
b 3
b 2
b 1
a 1
a 2
a 3
LEAVE SUFFICIENT LENGTH IN LEAD TWINE TO MAKE EVEN MESHES.
b 3
b 2
b 1
a 3
a 2
a 1

will be working in the regular method, but to net into meshes 1a, 2a, and 3a using the regular method it is necessary to turn the work. A quicker way is to use the technique described on page 59 under Pick-Up Knots.)

SMALL LOBSTER HEAD

The entrance to the kitchen section of the trap requires a somewhat smaller head. Using the same gauge, twine, and directions as for the parlor head, net 7 and 6, 1 and 10 for a pattern.

LOBSTER TRAP END

These ends vary depending on the size of the trap and according to individual preferece, but most are straight netting with a narrowing at each end on the next-to-last row so that the netted piece fits the contour of the trap. These directions are for the average parlor-style trap.

1. Take up 8 meshes on a $2^{1}/_{2}$-inch board, using heading twine or nylon twine #750. Use the chain start (page 19).

2. Net 6 rows, using the old-fashioned method (page 24).

3. Net the seventh row, but make a narrowing (page 30) on the second mesh and next-to-last mesh.

4. Net row 8 and end twine.

Attach to the trap by inserting a lath through the netting and nailing it to the trap.

Eel Traps and Nozzles

Eeling was particularly popular in Maine about the turn of the century, when the Scandinavian stonecutters migrated here to work in the quarries. Knowledgeable about the ways to catch eels, they were also skilled in the culinary arts of cooking them. A Swede might serve an eel jellied, smoked, grilled, fried, even as a canapé, with or without a touch of dill, but always as a delectable dish done to perfection.

They were just as versatile at catching an eel. Sometimes it seemed almost capricious. One might use a trap, a hook, a bob (a mesh of bait-laden thread in which the eel's teeth became entangled), a comb (a rakelike device that pierced the eel), or perhaps even an eel pen (a miniature weir strung across a small brook).

In the winter an eeler went out on the frozen ponds and carefully excavated what Downeasters call a "dry hole" by cutting a circle in the ice about a foot and a half in diameter. When he reached the last five inches of the circumference he would stop cutting and with a swift blow of the ax strike the piece in such a way that the entire circle broke off intact without leaving any ice chips to crowd the opening. He would then take the cleanly sheared disk and push it under the surface, storing it neatly under the floor of the ice. Next he would thrust his spear through the clear icy pool into the muddy nest below. The spear was long enough that he could reach across a fairly wide arc. If luck was with him (and it usually was) he caught an eel. When through for the day, he kept the hole open by stuffing it with a small fir tree and went home confident that no haphazard skater would accidentally fall in. A busy pond full of eelers took on the appearance of a miniature forest by spring.

Even though some biologists doubt the stories of eels traveling overland, many an old Swede on the island of Vinalhaven knew that in the fall, when the full-grown adults were ready to start the long migration home, they would come out of the Sands quarry, always on a rainy night and on the dark of the moon. If he were ready with his net he would catch them slithering down the rainy rivulets, new-filled puddles, and freshets across the stretch of muddy Sands road to reach the sea. Oldtimers vouch for the truth of this legend, and a check of Maine eel landings lends credence to the story when one finds that the largest catch of Maine eels has been in the fall during a heavy rain storm and on a moonless night.

Today the most common way to catch an adult eel in Maine is with a trap. Essentially an adaptation of a fyke net, this is a netted trap kept under tension (in this case by hoops). The design most popular Down East is a three-foot-long cylinder of wire mesh with a netted nozzle, or head, on either end. Some traps have a further pocket or additional nozzles inside, the mesh decreasing gradually into a cod-end, a funnel of netting in which fish gather. The cod-end can be closed or opened by an easily released knot. A small door at the middle or lower end provides access to attach bait or remove the imprisoned eel.

The important thing about any eel trap is the size of the mesh. Eels are powerful and can muster an enormous amount of strength to force their way out if they can nose into even a small opening. Any mesh larger than one-half-inch will allow the escape of a two-pound eel. An inch mesh might hold an eel several pounds or more but the catch will be limited.

Although a large foreign market exists for eels (and particularly elvers, the catching methods for which are not described here), Maine landings are very low. In 1920, Maine landings of eels were approximately 300,000 pounds, but in recent years the largest catch was in 1971, when only thirteen hundred pounds were recorded.* The population of eels apparently has not changed, but difficulties in marketing have made the eel fishery economically unfeasible. Smoked eels are in demand—particularly in the Scandinavian countries, Germany, and Japan—and the Maine Department of Marine Resources has conducted studies helpful to anyone interested in harvesting or marketing eels. Certainly a large potential market exists.

Figure 7-2. Eel trap.

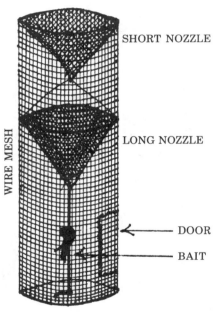

SHORT NOZZLE

LONG NOZZLE

WIRE MESH

DOOR

BAIT

---

*Farrin, Afton, "Observations, Facts, and Suggestions Regarding the American Eel (*Anguilla rostrata*)." Circular No. 29, Maine Department of Sea and Shore Fisheries.

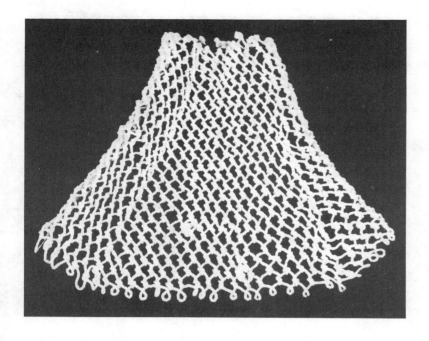

Short eel nozzle.

SHORT EEL NOZZLE

Use a ³/₄-inch mesh board and nylon twine #15. Work in the new-fashioned method, page 27.

1. Take up 18 meshes on a foundation loop (page 21).

2. Net 7 rows.

3. In the next row make 4 widenings (see page 30) by netting 4 meshes and widening one, netting 5 meshes and widening one, then 4 meshes and widen one, 5 meshes and widen one.

4. Net a plain row.

5. Net another row in which 4 widenings are placed under the previous ones.

6. Net a plain row.

7. Continue alternating a plain row and one in which 4 widenings have been placed under the previous ones until there are 56 meshes.

8. End twine. Remove foundation loop.

9. Lace to eel trap.

LONG EEL NOZZLE

Use a ³/₄-inch mesh board and nylon twine #15, and work in the new-fashioned method, page 27.

1. Take up 30 meshes on a foundation loop (page 21).

2. Net 2 plain rows.

3. On the third row, net 7 meshes and put in one widening (see page 30), net eight meshes and widen one, net 7 and widen one, net 8 and widen one.

4. Net a plain row.

5. Put in 4 widenings in the next row under the ones in the third row.

6. Net another plain row.

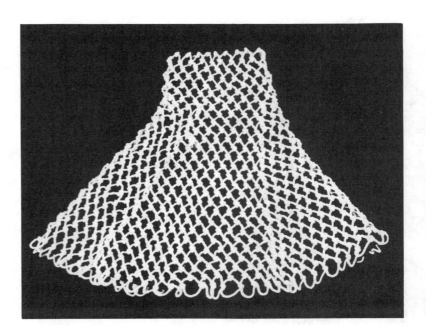

Long eel nozzle.

7. Continue alternating a row with 4 widenings and a plain row until there are 56 meshes.

8. End twine, remove foundation loop, and lace nozzle to ring. (This particular pattern fits a ring 45 inches in diameter.)

9. Lace to eel trap.

Dip, Hoop, and Fyke Nets

Dip Nets or Landing Nets

These nets come in many sizes, from what is called in Maine a "brailer" ("bailer" elsewhere), down to a minnow net. The essential purpose of the brailer is to lift already trapped fish from the water and into a fishing boat's hold. They are used when carrier pumps are not feasible or available. A brailers is a very large circular net with a long pole or stick attached. The stick is equipped with iron rings through which a rope is passed. By manipulating the rope, the bottom of the net may be opened and closed. When the full brailer is hoisted on deck, the ropes are worked to release the bottom of the net, discharging the fish into the hold.

Dip nets are used for multiple purposes: to scoop lobsters from a pound, take herring or pogies from a pocket, gather smelts in a brook, or (for kids) to catch minnows.

The two patterns given here are made in essentially the same way; that is, by starting a square base, as shown in the hand scallop drag (page 77) and the shopping bags (pages 48 and 49). The first one is made from nylon and is used for small fish, three-inch herring or smelt. The second one is included as an example of the netting that was typical of the island only a few years ago. It was made from cotton twine with a small mesh in the base graduating to larger meshes toward the top of the net. It was used for minnows, migrating elvers, and other very small fish. Both nets were attached to a circular frame with a handle, which may be purchased commercially.

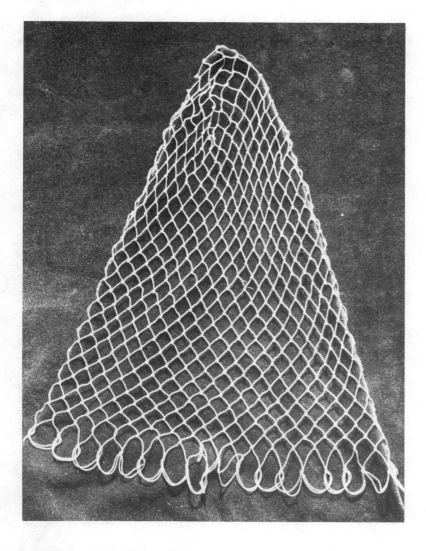

Smelt net. Charlotte Goodhue photo.

SMELT DIP NET

Use fine nylon twine #9 and $1^1/_4$-inch and 2-inch mesh boards. Work in either netting method (see pages 24 to 29).

1. Take up 7 meshes on the $1^1/_4$-inch board using either the chain start (page 19) or foundation loop (page 21).

2. Net 14 rows to make a rectangle.

3. Square the rectangle by widening one in each corner as shown in the Shopping Bag patterns (pages 48 and 49).

4. Net 28 rows.

5. Change to the 2-inch mesh board and net another row.

6. Put double twine on the needle and net the last row with double twine, still using the 2-inch board.

7. End twine. Remove foundation loop. Lace net onto a 15-inch diameter hoop.

FINE (MINNOW) DIP NET

Use fine nylon twine #9 and $1/2$-inch, $3/4$-inch, and 1-inch mesh boards. Work in the new-fashioned method, page 27.

1. Take up 10 meshes on a foundation loop (page 21) using the $1/2$-inch board.

2. Net 20 rows to make a rectangle.

3. Square the rectangle by increasing (widening) one mesh in each corner, as shown in the directions for the Shopping Bags (pages 48 and 49).

4. Net around the square in a spiral, putting a widening in every seventh mesh. You will see that you will be widening 8 times in the row. Continue to do this on every other row until there are 70 meshes.

5. Net 24 more rows without widening.

Minnow net made around 1920.
Charlotte Goodhue photo.

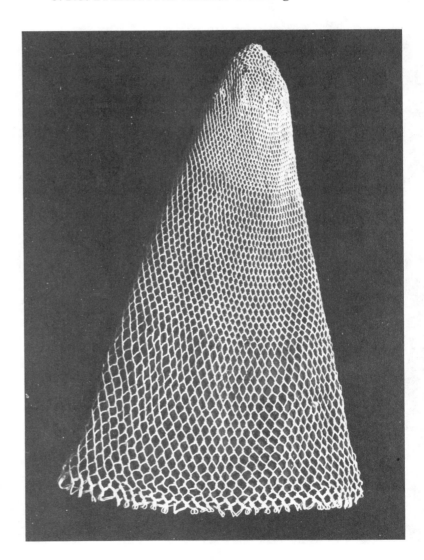

6. Change to the 3/4-inch board and net 22 rows.

7. Change to the 1-inch board and net 18 rows.

8. Double the twine on your needle and net two rows with double twine. End twine. With new twine net or lace onto frame.

Hoop Nets

In reality a form of dip net, hoop nets are used to actually catch fish instead of merely lifting them from the water. Their circumference varies, but can be as great as three yards. A large iron or steel ring forms the hoop, which often was (and sometimes still is) made from a discarded carriage or wagon wheel rim. The rim lasts a surprisingly long time without rusting away—often twenty-five to thirty years.

A bridle, usually ropes tied to the ring and crossed in the middle, holds the hoop net and a long cord with a float so that the submerged net may be located. The bait is hung from the bridle. A wooden toggle is tied at the bridle to give enough buoyancy so that it will not lay across the top of the net. Usually a heavy rock is used to weigh down the whole net assembly.

When the net is jerked quickly to the surface, the rock falls to the center of the net and creates more of a depression in the base, creating a sort of pocket and making it difficult for the prey to climb or swim out of the net before it reaches the surface. Flounder, crabs—and in the old days, even lobster—were caught by this method.

One of the drawbacks to the hoop net is that it must be lowered where fish are abundant, for although the bait may attract the prey, there is no real barrier to keep it trapped, and once the bait is devoured the crab, lobster, or flounder moves on. Even so, before bait came in truckloads to the island (consisting of trimmings from canning factories), the hoop net was the means by which many lobstermen obtained the bait for their pots. One fisherman tells of keeping eighty to ninety traps filled with flounder caught by a crab-baited hoop net. Who knows? Now that bait is in limited supply and the price sky-high, the hoop net may come back in style.

HOOP NET

Use nylon twine #36 or heading twine #750 and 2-inch and 3-inch mesh boards. This net can be made by either the old-fashioned or new-fashioned netting methods (pages 24 to 29.)

1. Using the 2-inch board, take up 7 meshes using either the chain start (page 19) or foundation loop (page 21) method.

2. Net 14 rows.

3. Square the corners in this section by putting one widening in each corner, as in the Shopping Bag patterns (pages 48 and 49).

4. Net a plain row in a spiral around the square.

5. Net 11 meshes and widen once, 11 more and widen

once; repeat the sequence twice more, so that there are 4 increases in the row.

6. Net a plain row.

7. Widen again 4 times in the next row, putting the widenings under the ones that were made previously.

8. Continue alternating plain and widening rows until there are 69 meshes.

9. Net 8 more rows in plain netting.

10. Net another row in double twine.

11. Change to the 3-inch mesh board and net the last row in double twine. End twine.

12. Attach to a 15-inch diameter steel ring by using a new length of twine to lace, hitch, or net all meshes to the ring.

Fyke Nets

Sometimes called hoop nets, although quite different from the hoop net already described, the fyke net is a series of netted pockets supported by rings or hoops. A drawstring at the smaller end releases the catch after it has been trapped in the maze of progressively smaller pockets. Tied to posts driven in the bottom of sand or mud, the nets are stationary, and in essence, resemble a weir. Their efficiency is augmented by wings that guide the fish toward the net.

The net pictured starts with a 1½-inch mesh, decreasing to one-inch as the pockets decrease in size. These nets

Fyke net. The long "wing" extending from the open end guides fish into the trap. Charlotte Goodhue photo.

are purchased commercially today. Their use on Vinalhaven has been confined to eels; however, fyke nets are used for other fish in river areas, placed so that fish are guided into the net.

Scallop Drags

Maine scallops are winter fare. Although most of the scallops caught are deep-sea scallops, a large percentage are actually caught inshore between November and April (after that, they must be caught in deeper waters). Quite often the drags are attached to lobster boats converted in winter to accommodate a drag and winch. Although the scallops are caught by towing a heavy drag, the boats are known as scallopers, not draggers.

Scalloping is dangerous, and this was tragically exemplified in 1977 and 1978 by deaths of scallopers from Cape Cod. A drag full of scallops, rocks, and mud, hoisted aboard a deck already weighted down with unshucked scallops, is

Scallop drag raised to go overboard. (John Morton in the *Barbara M.*) Charlotte Goodhue photo.

The iron rings extend partway up the side on this scallop drag. On the left-hand side of the drag as shown here, are the wooden "clubs" that close off the end of the bag. On the right-hand end is the Y-shaped bail. The cutter bar is underneath, not visible. Charlotte Goodhue photo.

unwieldy in a choppy, wind-tossed sea. A drag swung off-balance can quickly capsize a boat.

In the 1960s there were no scallop buyers on Vinalhaven, and my husband often came home with ice-covered eyebrows and beard only to face the chores of weighing, boxing, and selling his catch to sympathetic neighbors. But this hardship did not dim our delight when the scallop was dropped still quivering into a hot pan, and a fresh scallop, or a scallop that has been frozen shortly after the catch, is still one of our favorite foods. (Once, when we were anxious to share scallops with a New Yorker, we had the unexpected problem of convincing him that we did, in truth, have scallops; the sweet smell so characteristic of some market scallops is not present when the scallops are fresh.)

Some scallop drags are made completely from iron rings, but often, in order to reduce weight, a portion of the drag is netted. Netted sections vary. The bottom of the drag, which is hauled across the ocean floor, is usually made from iron rings, while the upper section of the drag is netted. In some cases, as in the photograph, the rings are partially carried over into the upper section.

When the net is made, the needle used is open-ended and wide so that rope can be easily wound around it. A full needle almost resembles a ball. The material used is a heavy rope, such as float rope or similar polyethylene, 1/4 or 3/8 inch in diameter. The finished piece is netted or laced into rings or connectors on the cutter bar.

Another method to make the net is a form of knotless netting. The rope is wound around nails that form a jig, or

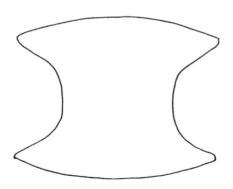

Figure 7-3. Scallop drag needle.

Sometimes metal clips are used instead of knots on scallop drags. Charlotte Goodhue photo.

template, for the netted section. Metal clips join the meshes instead of knots.

There is no formula for depth or mesh size, for scallop drags vary according to the individual rig. All are made essentially as described.

Simple hand drags are used if a fisherman would like a "mess" of scallops for supper. The one illustrated was found in the late Birger Magnuson's fish house. The cutter bars and bail have been forge welded, so this drag dates probably from the early 1900s. Although there is a slight slant to the bail, designating a top and a bottom, the double cutter bars enabled it to fish however it happened to land when it struck bottom. It was thrown haphazardly overboard from the stern of a dory and pulled along the bottom as the fisherman rowed.

The netted section of this drag was started by a single chain of thirty 3¼-inch meshes, and the corners were "squared" by one widening in each corner. These 34 meshes were netted in a helix for 14 rows. The net was attached to the cutter bar by a new length of twine, which was put through the holes in the bar and netted into the mesh in the main section with a one-inch mesh board.

Toggles

Toggles made by covering glass quart bottles were common in the past, but as more boats became equipped with mechanical pot haulers, the breakable glass toggles became less popular. Such toggles are still seen, but much less frequently. The toggle illustrated is quick and easy to make:

Birger Magnuson's scallop drag, made in the early 1900s. Charlotte Goodhue photo.

Toggle. Charlotte Goodhue photo.

Two quart bottles are placed end to end, covered with a tube of netting, and the ends laced tightly at either neck. The meshes are large, so the old-fashioned netting method lends itself well here.

Use heading twine #550 or #750 and a 4-inch mesh board.

1. Take up 4 meshes using the chain start (page 19) and net 7 rows.

2. Connect each row by netting the first and the last strand together.

3. Leave a tail at both beginning and end to lace around the bottle necks.

Torch, Purse, and Stop Seines

Torch Seining

Currently illegal in Maine, torch seining is perhaps the most dramatic way to catch fish. It was used almost exclusively to catch herring and took place always after dark.

Rowing around a likely cove in the darkness, the men look for the water to "fire." This is a flash of phosphorescence when the water is disturbed and indicates an abundance of plankton, on which herring feed. The fishermen would pole the water in a cove by standing in the bow of a dory and dipping a long pole to feel for the movement of fish. (An electrical fish finder is used today, but poling is still practiced to some extent.) Once a school of fish was located, the men moved into position to set the net.

Quietly, so not to disturb the fish, a net would be extended across the mouth of the cove, in a slightly drifting curve, between two dories. The net would be bellied to form a large pocket, one side having a float line to keep it above water, the other side leaded so it would sink and open. An added weight on each end helped keep the net in place. Each dory was equipped with a small flashlight so that a third man in a peapod could spot the line of twine across the mouth of the cove.

Then the fun began! Attached to the bow of a peapod was a metal dip net or wire-mesh ball filled with gasoline-soaked crocus bags. Starting well back in the cove behind the twine, a third fisherman lit this torch and started rowing quickly toward the center of the net, guided by the small specks of light from the dories at either end. The fish, attracted by the fire, would swim toward it. As the peapod gained momentum, the fish would quicken their pace and become frenzied as hundreds and then thousands of herring swam, jumped, and flipped in an insane stampede to follow the torch. Often the rower's oars would become useless as he neared the net, trying desperately to row through a sea of fish.

As the rower finally crossed the net, the two end men would tighten the twine, pulling the leaded side up to make a pocket to hold the catch. The fish would later be pumped or brailed from the net. In most cases they were used for bait.

Pictured is a small torch seine used on Vinalhaven. A close look at the photograph will show the side end weights,

A torch seine formerly used to catch herring. The float line is on the left, with cork floats, and the lead line lies a couple of feet to the right. Charlotte Goodhue photo.

the float line, and the lead line. The catch in this net can be twenty to twenty-five bushels at a set.

Purse Seines and Stop Seines

Purse seines are not apt to be used in coves but from large boats in the open ocean. The fish are spotted and surrounded by many fathoms of twine. Heavy lead lines speed the sinking of the net. A purse string threaded through brass rings is hauled tightly to close the net along the bottom, and the vertical sides are pulled to tighten the enclosure. These are commercially made nets.

Stop seines are set across the mouth of a cove in a slight arc, the same as the torch seine, but instead of being held by dories they are firmly attached on either shore, preferably above the high water mark. They, too, have the float line and the weighted lead line and form a curtain barrier that prevents fish from leaving the cove.

Once the fish are held behind the barrier, a pocket is attached to the outer side of the twine and the float line adjacent to the pocket is lowered by using sinking rocks or weights. The fish, trying to escape through this apparent breach in the net, are channeled instead into the pocket and are trapped.

The fine-meshed stop seines and purse seines are made on commercial looms and purchased from net or twine companies, but although fishermen buy them ready-made,

This photo, taken off Matinicus Island, shows fishermen seining the pocket outside the original float line. Courtesy of Isabel Osgood.

the damage to these nets from hauling, weather and tide, and hungry dogfish or seals is often extensive, and fishermen spend many hours net-mending, patching, and lacing.

Gill Nets

Once made from linen twine, gill nets are today made from monofilament, a single strand of clear synthetic that is almost invisible under water. Some are dyed to match the varying shades of the ocean, and schools of fish approaching the net have little warning of what is ahead. If the net is tight, the fish detect the barrier with their built-in sonar sense, but if the net is slack and drifting (as well as being invisible), the fish swim into the net unaware of danger. In fact, gill nets are often called drift nets.

The looseness of the mesh is augmented by not tying every mesh to the float line. Instead, the net is hung at inter-

Robin Adair hanging a gill net. Charlotte Goodhue photo.

vals so that a certain amount of slackness exists when the net is drifting. The fine twine catches the fish behind the gills, preventing it from moving forward or backward, and the more it thrashes in an attempt to escape, the more it becomes entangled in the net.

Gill nets are rarely netted but are purchased already made. Different size meshes exist for different size fish, and the fisherman usually orders the mesh size to correspond to the catch he hopes to encounter. For example, someone fishing for haddock would buy a 4- to 4½-inch mesh, but for groundfish one would purchase a 5½-inch mesh. When selecting a gill net, the buyer looks for netting with the lowest visibility, softness to reduce sound waves, strength enough to prevent fish from breaking the mesh, and sufficient elasticity that the mesh will return to size after the fish are removed.

After the net is purchased, it must be hung on a float line, to hold the top of the net, and a lead line (a rope with a core of lead) to sink the bottom. This ensures that although the net will drift to a large degree it will still represent a wall-like barrier for the school of fish.

Gill nets must hang and not simply be tied or lashed to the line. This is accomplished by catching up the meshes at intervals along the float line. If the net is hung on a one-third basis, the twine is run through three meshes and then hitched to the float line. If hung on a one-half basis, four meshes are picked up on the twine before hitching it to the line. In either case, the distance between the hitches is only that of two stretched meshes. A chart showing number of meshes needed is shown for one-half and one-third basis.

The twine is attached to the first two meshes, giving added strength and leaving a line of meshes at the side for the frame end—a rope laced down the side of the mesh. Corks or floats are threaded into the float line about a fathom apart, or every six feet. The net is attached to the float line either by

Chart E: One-Half Basis Netting Chart
Number of meshes needed to hang different depths (in feet).

FEET DEEP	SQUARE STRETCH	1" Sq. 2" Str.	1¼" Sq. 2½" Str.	1½" Sq. 3" Str.	1¾" Sq. 3½" Str.	2" Sq. 4" Str.	2¼" Sq. 4½" Str.	2½" Sq. 5" Str.	2¾" Sq. 5½" Str.	3" Sq. 6" Str.	3¼" Sq. 6½" Str.	3½" Sq. 7" Str.	3¾" Sq. 7½" Str.	4" Sq. 8" Str.	4½" Sq. 9" Str.	5" Sq. 10" Str.	SQUARE STRETCH
3 ft.		20	16	13	11	10	9	8	7	6	6	5	5	5	4	4	
3½ ft.		23	19	16	13	12	10	9	8	8	7	6	6	5	5	4	
4 ft.		27	22	18	15	13	12	11	10	9	8	8	7	7	6	5	
5 ft.		34	27	22	19	17	15	13	12	11	10	9	9	8	7	6	
6 ft.		41	32	27	23	20	18	16	15	13	12	11	11	10	9	8	
7 ft.		47	38	32	27	24	21	19	17	16	14	13	12	12	10	9	
8 ft.		54	44	36	31	27	24	21	20	18	16	15	14	13	12	11	
10 ft.		68	54	45	39	34	30	27	24	22	21	19	18	17	15	13	
12 ft.		82	65	54	46	41	36	32	30	27	25	23	21	20	18	16	
14 ft.		95	76	63	54	47	42	38	34	31	29	27	25	24	21	19	
16 ft.		109	87	72	62	54	48	43	39	36	33	31	29	27	24	21	
18 ft.		122	98	82	70	61	54	49	44	41	37	35	32	30	27	24	
20 ft.		136	109	91	78	68	60	54	49	45	42	39	36	34	30	27	

MESH SIZE

• **HOW TO READ CHART:** Example — To hang 6' deep, net of 2" square mesh — Use 20 mesh deep netting. See circled example above.

(Courtesy of Nylon Net Company)

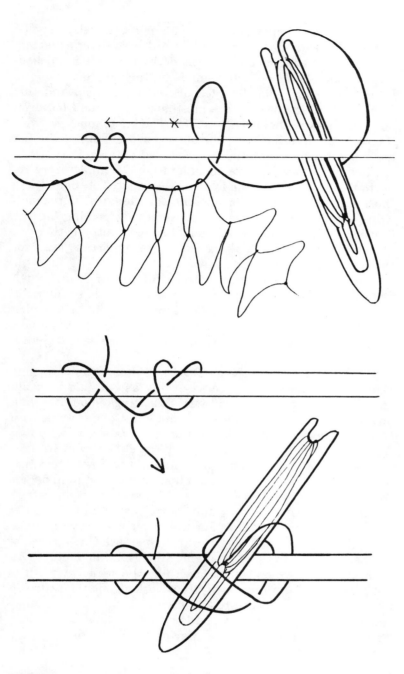

Figure 7-4. Hanging a gill net with clove hitches. The distance between hitches is equal to 2 stretched meshes.

Figure 7-5. Making the rolling hitch. Lay the twine on the head–rope, go down and to the back, then around to the front and cross the end of the twine. Make 2 more turns around the rope, then bring the twine to the front, going under both of the last 2 turns.

a series of half-hitches [*Figure 7-4*] or by a more binding rolling hitch [*Figure 7-6*]. These are shown with the position of the needles so that they may be made more easily.

Netting Together a Commercially Purchased Net

A trawl is basically a long conical net that is dragged along the bottom. The cone's tip, which holds the catch, is called the cod end. The top of the net is called the square, and the middle section, the belly. The wide mouth of the net is often held open by wooden doors, and it has winglike ends to guide the fish into the net.

Large nets, such as beam or shrimp trawls, may be purchased ready-made or made to order at several netting factories, but they also can be made by the individual fisherman from sheets of factory-made netting. If that case, the first consideration is the type of netting to use, and this means selecting not only the mesh size, color, and material but also the way the mesh is woven. The knots must go "with the run," as described on page 56 under Mending. If the net has been interwoven, braided, or welded to make it knotless, obviously the run is not a consideration. Manufacturers refer to the width across the loom as the "depth" of the net and the number of rows of meshes as the "length." Often machines make the knot across the depth. Depending on the finished net size required, one might have to butt together two lengths of net, so netmaking skills are important even for those who use the machine-woven nets.

Another consideration is that the machines make selvedges along the length but not across the depth. In adding a selvedge, one can net over the end mesh and make a double row, or add a heavier twine along the edge by netting an new row, in which case the net is increased by one row, or half a mesh.

When cutting patterns from purchased netting, one should spread out the piece as evenly as possible to avoid making mistakes on the meshes. The wings should be laid out so that the widest end is the first cut. Colored twine run through where the cut helps in lining up. Lower wings often line up so that they will cut along a line of bars in a straight slant, but upper wings have one side that will not accommodate this angle of cut. The cuts must be planned to allow for the fact that meshes are "lost" when one cuts into a net. In cutting the lower wing, it will be obvious that half a mesh of netting is lost on each row. For the wider and varying shape of the upper wing, one might have to increase the number of meshes in a row to compensate for this loss. If in doubt, leave an extra mesh, which can be laced into the seam later if it is not needed. (Formulas have been worked out for tapering nets, and anyone interested in pursuing this topic further can send to the University of Rhode Island for *Cutting Web Tapers*, by Geoffrey A. Motte, Marine Leaflet Series no. 1.)

8 Other Practical Projects

SCARF

This scarf is designed to fit easily inside an open collar and is made of fine fingering yarn for warmth and lightness. (Longer scarves may be made by netting more rows.) There is no fringe on this scarf, for its purpose is only to shut out the wind with a minimum of bulk when the top button on a winter coat is left open.

Use care when netting with yarn, for the knots are difficult to remove to undo a mistake, and it can be tricky to maintain even meshes if the wool stretches.

Use 1¾-inch mesh board, a medium-sized netting needle, and 2 one-ounce balls of fingering yarn. Work in either

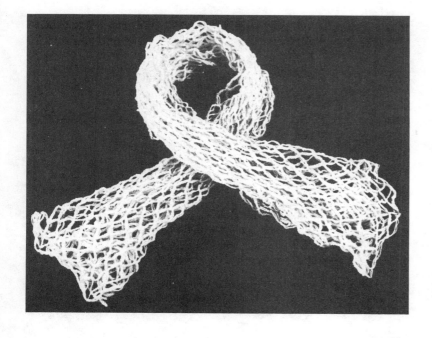

Netted scarf.
Charlotte Goodhue photo.

the new-fashioned or old-fashioned netting method (pages 24 to 29).

1. Double the yarn when winding the needle by taking from two balls of yarn simultaneously.
2. Pick up 26 meshes on a foundation loop (page 21).
3. Net 35 rows down and tie off the end.
4. Remove the foundation loop.

TENNIS NETS

Game regulations call for uniformity and rigidity in tennis nets. For this reason, square meshes are used instead of diamonds. Although the length of the net may vary—36 feet for lawn tennis, 33 for singles and 42 for doubles—the mesh size is always $1^{1}/_{2}$ inches. Lawn tennis nets are usually 42 inches deep, while the other two are 36 inches. A $2^{1}/_{2}$-inch plastic or canvas strip is sewn to the top of the net in which a wire cable, $^{1}/_{3}$-inch in diameter, is inserted. The bottom may be finished with a strip of plastic or canvas or else hitched to a rope, leaving ends that are later tied to supporting side posts.

These large-meshed nets may be worked in either the old-fashioned or new-fashioned netting method (pages 24 to 29), and are usually made from #36 cotton twine.

PING-PONG, OR TABLE TENNIS, NET

Ping Pong nets also have a square mesh, but each side of the mesh is only half an inch. Make the net six feet long and six inches deep. Use #36 cotton twine and work in the new-fashioned method. Finish the top and bottom by sewing on a plastic or canvas strip, leaving long enough ends to tie the net to posts.

BASKETBALL NET

This net is made either directly onto the frame by taking up the meshes on the circular holder at the start, or it is net separately and the completed net hooked into the notches provided on some frames. Use either old-fashioned or new-fashioned netting (pages 24 to 30) and #72 cotton twine.

To make a net 18-inches in circumference, take up 11 meshes, leaving a tail end about two feet long. If the holder has notches, use an 8-inch mesh board for the first row, but if if you are taking up the meshes directly onto the frame, use a $9^{1}/_{2}$-inch board. Tie the net together with the tail end at the end of each row, just as for the Thermos Bottle Cover (page 45). You will notice that there are now 12 meshes.

Change to a 3-inch mesh board and net the second row. Continuing with the 3-inch board, net rows 3, 4, 5, and 6, and end the twine by making a single overhand knot in the end of the lead twine and in the tail adjacent to the last netting knot. These knots help secure the netting so that it will not unravel with hard usage.

POOL TABLE POCKETS

Small orders still come to the island for pool pockets, but they were more in demand sixty years ago. In those days payment was $1.25 per hundred. The common quip heard in regard to the meager payment is that it bought a lot more groceries then!

You can easily repair the worn-out pocket in your own table by making it similarly to the Glass Float Cover on page 43. Take up 13 meshes, net down 5 rows, draw together with a slip knot, as shown in the float cover instructions, and net it together, making 14 meshes around the pocket. Work in either old-fashioned or new-fashioned netting (pages 24 to 29) and use #16 cotton twine. Match the mesh size to the pocket size of your own pool table (see Planning the Net, page 16).

LAUNDRY BAG

This serviceable bag will withstand hard wear. The one pictured has seen better days but is still in use. It is made from heavy cord (almost as heavy as venetian-blind cord), and its rugged quality makes it an ideal carrier for things other than laundry. Having a drawstring at the bottom as well as the top allows easy access from either end.

Except for the addition of the second drawstring, this is made the same way as the Glass Float Cover (page 43) but on a larger scale. The bag can be worked in either old-fashioned or new-fashioned netting.

Use a 2-inch mesh board and nylon twine #96, or cotton cord.

1. Take up 34 meshes and net down for 44 rows.
2. Net the last row with double twine.
3. Put a drawstring through the bottom meshes and pull it tight so that the piece may be turned and netted together.
4. Turn, and net the sides. End the twine.
5. Complete the top by threading another drawstring through the meshes.

HAMMOCK

Usually hammocks are made from heavy cotton twine. Although cotton is not as durable as nylon, its softness is a decided asset when one is enjoying the luxury of an outdoor nap. The mesh size for a hammock is a matter of choice; anything from 1 1/2 to 3 inches works well. A good-sized hammock has at least a three-foot spread and is eight or nine feet long.

All hammock patterns are essentially rectangular. Those formerly used aboard ships were often a straight rectangle, gathered at both ends and seized to metal rings. However, a hammock is actually more comfortable and easier to manipulate if the body section is made wider than the ends, making a deeper pocket to hold body weight. It also is preferable to spread the ends of the hammock with rods, which serve to keep the net open.

Use heading twine #750, nylon twine #48 (one-pound

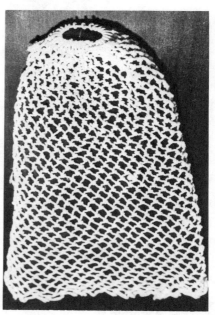

Laundry bag.
Charlotte Goodhue photo.

Lance Morton relaxing in a rope
hammock. Charlotte Goodhue photo.

ball), or cotton cable seine twine #36, and a 3-inch mesh
board. You will also need: two 3-inch iron rings (the ones
shown came from a scallop drag), 2 spreaders measuring 2
inches by 3 inches by 31 inches long (I used scrap oak table
legs), and about 17 feet of half-inch nylon rope.

If you use nylon twine, as shown here, a reinforced
selvedge is not usually necessary; the outside rope edge is
enough. If you do desire a stronger edge, though, make a
selvedge by taking in the outside thread with the first knot
netted on each row (see Selvedges, page 53).

1. Make the spreaders first. With the 3-inch side facing
up, drill sixteen ¼-inch holes, 1½ inches apart, through each
strip of wood, starting ¾-inch from the center and working
out to the edges. (The diameter of the holes may vary according to the type of twine used. Two strands must fit through

each hole.) The 14 inner holes are used for the bights of the clew (the lines from which the hammock is suspended), and the two outer holes are used for the heavier outer cord that is laced through the sides of the hammock for support.

2. Countersink the holes to minimize eventual wear and tear, then stain and varnish the wood.

3. The clew is made on a jig. Use a piece of scrap plywood about one yard square with a two-by-four nailed across the top. Center a large finish nail in the two-by-four and hang an iron ring on it. Measure 18 inches from the lower inner edge of the ring toward the bottom edge of the plywood. This is where you will place the nails that hold the bights of the clew, but first, nail down another two-by-four at this level, parallel to the upper two-by-four. Nail 14 finish nails across the bottom two-by-four, spaced two inches apart in a slight arc. The slight curvature will aid in making your bights come out even. (The example shown in Figure 8-1 shows a simpler version with only 6 bights to the clew.)

4. For this hammock, allow approximately 22 yards of twine for the clew. Leave a 2-foot tail and start at the left by leading the twine under the ring, down and around the first of the 14 nails from left to right, through the ring from underneath, down to loop around the second nail, and so forth. Be sure to always go around the nails from left to right. Continue until all the nails are looped and then bring the twine up through the ring, leave another 2-foot tail, and cut the twine.

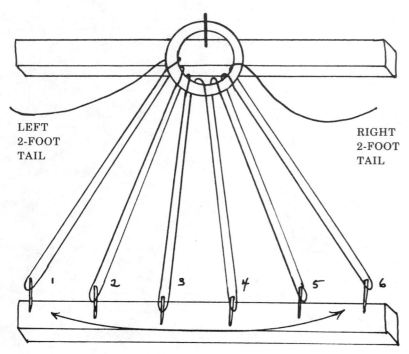

Figure 8-1. A clew set up with 6 bights, ready to weave.

LEFT
2-FOOT
TAIL

RIGHT
2-FOOT
TAIL

NAILS SET IN A SLIGHT ARC

This view shows the woven end of the bight. Charlotte Goodhue photo.

5. The two tails are now woven through the fan-shaped array of bights. Think of the strands wrapped around the ring and nails as the warp on a loom—in this case, a warp with 28 strands. The two loose ends are woven through these warp strands in a simple over one, under one pattern. With each weft row, a strand on the outside is skipped, however, and the end result will be a pointed woven reinforcement just below the iron ring.

The netting needle makes the task of weaving easier. Thread the needle with the right-hand tail and (working now from right to left) pass it under the first strand of the first bight, over the second strand of the same bight, over the next strand (the first one of the second bight), under the next strand, etc. Continue all the way across, but stop before the last strand. Don't pull the needle all the way through; instead, turn it on edge to create a space (the "shed," in weaver's terminology) between the upper and lower warp strands.

6. Next, pick up the left-hand tail on a second netting needle and work across from left to right, going over the first strand, under the next strand. Then pass the second tail through the shed formed by the first netting needle, again stopping one strand short of the end. Note that both strands go through the same shed; that is, they go over and under *the same* warp strands.

Figure 8-2. Weaving the bight.

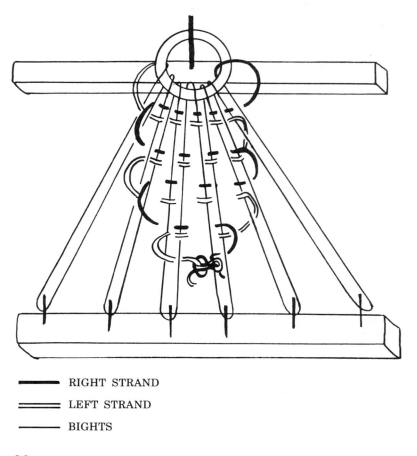

——— RIGHT STRAND

≡≡≡ LEFT STRAND

——— BIGHTS

7. Pull both tails all the way through and push them up toward the ring as snugly as possible. The first tail (shown in black in the illustration) is now on the left and is the upper of the two weft strands. Always work with this tail first, keeping it above the second tail.

8. Working with the first tail again, skip the first strand on the left, go over the second strand, under the third, and so on across the row. Stop at the second strand from the end. Turn the needle to make a shed and bring the second tail through, going under the second strand from the right, over the next strand, and through the shed. Pull the strands all the way through and push the newly woven strands up toward the ring.

9. Continue weaving this pattern as established until you reach the center. Secure the two tails with a reef knot (page 36) and melt the ends of the twine to prevent raveling.

10. Take the clew off the jig and thread the bights through the 14 center holes in one of the spreaders, leaving the 2 outer holes free for now. Make a second clew just like the first and thread it onto the second spreader bar.

11. Hang one of the clew assemblies by its iron ring and commence working the body of the hammock by netting across the loops that protrude through the spreader bar. Work with either the new-fashioned or old-fashioned netting method (pages 24 to 29).

12. Work 3 rows across. Increase one mesh (page 30, Widening) in the center of the fourth row. Net a plain row. In the sixth row, make 2 increases, one on either side of the first increase. Net another plain row, and on the eighth row again make 2 increases, each just to the outside of the preceding 2 increases.

13. Continue to net plain rows until the hammock is about 8 rows short of the desired length—typically 8 to 9 feet.

14. Decrease two meshes (page 30, Narrowing) on the eighth row from the end, with the decreases corresponding to the increases made at the beginning of the net on row 8. Decrease 2 more meshes on the sixth row from the end and one mesh on the fourth row from the end. Net 3 plain rows.

15. Hang the other clew assembly by its ring and net the last row of the hammock onto the loops protruding through the second spreader bar. This may be done by netting in reverse, but an easier method is to turn over the netting and work across, catching up the loops of the lower bight as if they were the meshes of a previously netted row.

16. Now that the body of the hammock is complete and attached to the clews, it is time to add the reinforcement rope along the edge. Take the length of half-inch rope and thread it through an end hole in the top spreader, knotting the end toward the ring so it will not pull out. Thread the other end of the rope through all the outside meshes along one side of the hammock and out through the end hole on the bottom spreader. Knot the rope again on the lower side of the spreader bar. Repeat the process on the other side.

Rachel Dwyer enjoys a netted swing. Charlotte Goodhue photo.

NETTED SWING

This swing is comfortable, easy to make, attractive, and ideal on the porch or under the apple tree.

Use 2 balls of heading twine #750 in a bright color and a 2½-inch mesh board. You will also need some cord for lacing through the outer edges of the swing—approximately 5 yards of cotton or #96 nylon cord.

Work in old-fashioned netting (page 24).

1. Using the chain start (page 19), take up 42 meshes.

2. Net down 81 rows. End by knotting and melting the cut end of the twine.

3. Fold the net in half along its shorter axis. Starting at the center fold on the right outer edge, net the strip together

for 23 meshes, leaving the remaining 18 meshes on each end open. This forms the seat pocket of the swing. For netting together, use the method described on page 43 under Glass Float Cover.

4. Take a 2-inch dowel 36 inches long and drill 2 holes through it at each end. One hole should be an inch from the end and the second 3 inches from the end. The holes should be large enough to accommodate a double thickness of the heavy cord used to suspend the swing.

5. Insert an end of the cord through the inner hole on one end of the dowel. Thread through the meshes on the front (open) edge of the swing and bring the end up through the inner hole on the other end of the dowel.

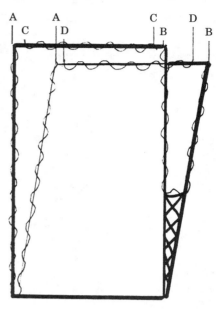

Figure 8-3. Insert cord through meshes in front (A to A). Insert cord through meshes in back (B to B). Gather ends (C–C and D–D).

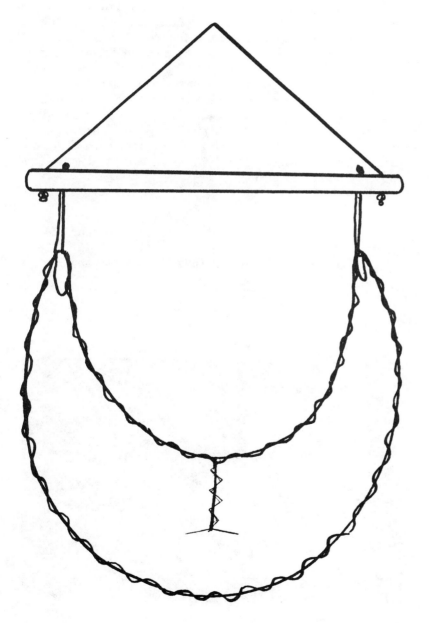

Figure 8-4.

6. Repeat this process along the back edge (the side with the pocket). (Note: the photo on page 92 shows a different hanging arrangement, but this way is stronger.)

7. With another length of cord, gather the meshes at one end of the swing, pull the loop tight, and tie off the cord. Repeat for the other end.

8. Take another length of cord long enough to suspend the swing at the level you desire and thread it through the outer holes of the dowel. Knot it securely on the underside of the dowel. Hang the swing, and once you've found a soft pillow to put in the bottom, you're all set!

Placemats

These attractive placemats lend a seacoast charm to a table setting. One tip: prevent excess joining knots by putting as much twine on your needle as is feasible. If a joining must appear, it is less conspicuous on the edge of the mat than in the center.

These mats need to be starched and stretched before use. Soak the mats well in water to preshrink them, then dip them in a laundry-starch solution and pin in place to dry. Pinning the outside meshes to a piece of pressed board works nicely. When the mats are dry brush them with urethane varnish on both sides. They will resist soil for a long time and may be rinsed off easily.

PLACEMAT I

Use cotton cable cord and a 3/4-inch mesh board. Work in new-fashioned netting (page 27).

1. Take up 38 meshes with the chain start (page 19).
2. Net down 28 rows.
3. Tie off.

Placemat. Charlotte Goodhue photo.

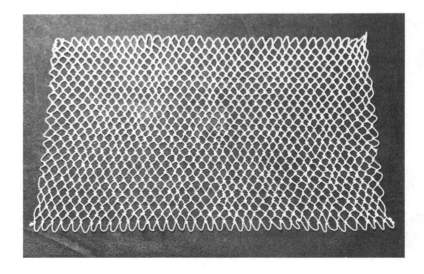

Placemat with double selvedge
before being stretched and
starched. Charlotte Goodhue photo.

PLACEMAT II

This pattern uses heavier twine and a larger mesh than the version above, so it can be worked in either old-fashioned or new-fashioned netting (pages 24 to 30). It has a decorative double selvedge on the long sides.

Use cotton cable cord and a 1¹/₂-inch mesh board.

1. Using double twine, take up 20 meshes with the chain start (page 19).

2. Change to single twine and net down 18 rows.

3. Change back to double twine and net the last row.

4. Tie off.

An example of fancy netting
made by the late Bernice Hall.
Charlotte Goodhue photo.

The late Flossie Williams
made this netted doily.
Charlotte Goodhue photo.

9 Fancy Netting

Every now and then netters take a break from the practical side of their work to create decorative articles, doing what can only be called "fancy netting." A few examples are shown here to illustrate the versatility of netting, and if you have mastered the basic skills demonstrated in the previous

A fanciful netting project is this fish sculpture. Courtesy of Bill Epton.

This fancy-netted evening bag was made by the late Mae Lawry. Valerie Morton photo.

chapters, you might want to try some of the more intricate meshes given at the end of this chapter, reprinted from *"The Young Ladies' Journal" Complete Guide to the Work-Table.*

The two doilies were both made by people on Vinalhaven. The first one was netted by the late Bernice Hall, and the second by the late Flossie Williams, who at eighty-eight was still busy at the net stand. The late Mae Lawry netted the evening bag. The fish, actually a piece of netted sculpture, was made by a summer resident, Bill Epton, and has been on exhibit in various galleries.

Instructions for several fancy-netting projects follow: Netted Curtains, Vanity Bag, and Horse Nets.

NETTED CURTAINS

These curtains decorate a window, give a sense of privacy, and help diffuse bright sunlight. The pattern looks quite different depending on how the curtain is hung; when turned and hung from the side, the mesh is elongated, giving a lacy effect. The variation in this pattern is accomplished merely by using a different size of mesh board, but more elaborate textures may be made with any of the fancy netting patterns reproduced at the end of this chapter. The finished curtain measures 36 inches deep when hung as netted, 76 inches when hung from the side, and of course the dimensions can be varied easily to fit a particular window.

Use $3/4$-inch and 2-inch mesh boards and #9 cotton twine. Work in either old-fashioned or new-fashioned netting (pages 24 to 29).

1. With the $3/4$-inch mesh board, take up 115 meshes and net down 4 rows. (You will have 5 rows of knots.)

2. Net one row on the 2-inch mesh board.

3. Net 5 rows on the $3/4$-inch board.

4. Continue netting one row on the 2-inch board and 5 rows on the $3/4$-inch board until you have netted 60 rows.

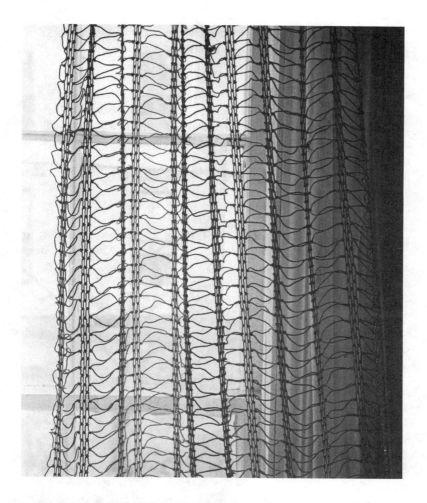

Netted curtain hung from the side.
Charlotte Goodhue photo.

Netted curtain hung as netted.
Charlotte Goodhue photo.

5. End with a group of 5 smaller-mesh rows to balance the 5 rows at the beginning of the piece. End twine.

VANITY BAG

The vanity bag is net similarly to the Bait Bag (page 46) but made from fine thread, and the fancy variation is achieved by omitting one mesh and netting into the next one, then returning and netting the omitted mesh.

Use fine thread, for this bag should be soft and collapsible; a soft crochet cotton, Clark's #30, works well. The purpose of the bag is to be able to hide rings or other valuables when traveling. Be sure to use a firm drawstring that is strong enough to tie securely.

Use ½- and ¾-inch mesh boards and the smallest-size needle shown on page 8. Work with the new-fashioned netting technique (page 27).

1. Using the ¾-inch mesh board, take up 30 meshes on a Net the next row, widening one mesh (page 30) in every other mesh, and connect the bag by netting in a spiral (page 42).

2. Net a plain row.

3. Net the next row, widening once in every fifth mesh.

4. Net 4 rows in plain netting.

5. On the next row, skip the first mesh and net the second. Return and net the first mesh. Skip the third mesh and net the fourth. Return and net the third mesh. Continue across the row in this fashion, skipping one mesh and net-

Made of fine mesh, this vanity bag holds rings, money, or other valuables while traveling. It was tied to garters or girdle. Charlotte Goodhue photo.

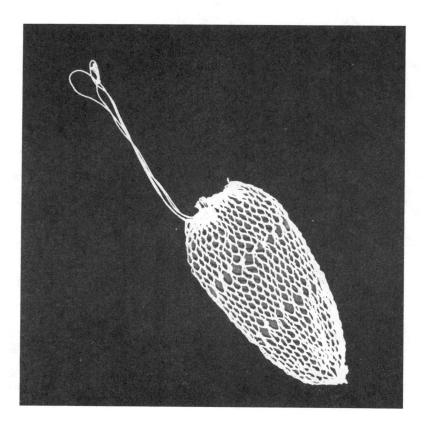

ting the next, returning to the skipped mesh and netting it. This crosses the meshes.

6. Net 7 more rows in plain netting.

7. Net another row, skipping the meshes and then netting them, as you did before.

8. Net 7 more rows in plain netting.

9. Change to a $3/4$-inch mesh board and net the last row with double twine. End twine and insert a drawstring. The finished bag will be about 6 inches long.

Horse Nets: Fly Net and Bonnet

The horse net in the photograph is one of the few remaining original nets from the Vinalhaven net factory. Loaned by Libby Magnuson, it is shown adorning the horse of our island doctor, Greg O'Keefe. Horse nets vary according to their use. The pattern given below is for a riding horse. It has two sets of tassels. The net in the photograph has spaces left for the traces, so it appears to be for a carriage horse. It is decorated with three rows of tassels.

Lance Morton photo.

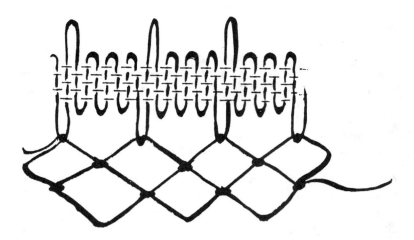

Figure 9-1 Starting the net on the woven band.

These nets were started on a woven band one inch wide and as long as the horse from withers to top of tail. The band is woven with regularly-spaced loops along the sides, and these serve as the net's foundation loops. If you choose to try making a horse fly net—and they are great for parades as well as to keep the flies away—you will need to have a weaver friend make the band. It is a regular tabby weave, but with one-inch loops made from the weft thread at 1¼-inch intervals along the selvedges. [*See figure 9-1.*]

FLY NET

Use #9 or #12 cotton or nylon twine and 2-inch and 4-inch mesh boards. For the crocheted chains use #36 cotton twine. Work in either old-fashioned or new-fashioned netting.

You will need a woven center band one inch wide and 50 inches long, with 40 one-inch foundation loops on each side. (Length of band and number of meshes can be adjusted according to size of horse.)

Run a long half-inch dowel through the loops on one side of the woven band and hang it from wall-mounted hooks set at about chest level. Start netting on the loops along the lower edge of the band. Turn the work as you complete each row.

Row 1. Using the 2-inch mesh board, net across the forty foundation loops.

Row 2. Widen one mesh (page 30) on the second mesh, net across the row, and widen again once on the next-to-last mesh.

Rows 3 through 15. Continue netting as established.

Row 16. Net across the row. Turn the work, and net across the same row a second time, but this time net into every other mesh and use the 4-inch mesh board. (If you do not have a mesh board this large, use the 2-inch board and wrap the twine around twice.) This extra row of large meshes forms the loops for hanging tassels.

Row 17. Again working across the main body of the net and using the 2-inch mesh board, net across the row.

Row 18. If you choose to vary the colors of your net, tie on the second color at this point. Net across the row.

Rows 19 through 26. Continue netting as established.

Row 27. Change back to the 4-inch mesh board and net across on row. Tie off.

Turn over the work and repeat all rows on the other side of the center band. Rethreading the dowel through the opposite side of the center band will keep it out of the way as you work the second half of the net.

This net will drape over the horse from the mane to the top of the tail. It is secured in two places: below the tail and around the chest. For the front ties, a crocheted cotton chain is threaded through the edge meshes of the net—beginning at row 16, up through and over the top, and down to row 16 on the other side. The ends (usually 8 inches long) tie either beneath or in front of the horse's breast. The front chain should be about 5 feet long overall, depending on the size of the horse.

Another crocheted chain is threaded along the rear edge of the net, but it forms a continuous span across from row 16 to row 16 (no extra bows or ties are under the tail). The tied ends, if any, are at the top. The tail chain is usually about 4 feet long, depending on the size of the horse.

Fly nets were traditionally decorated with tassels. In this pattern the tassels are attached to that extra row of large meshes at row 16 and to the last row of meshes. Along the bottom edge, loop each tassel through 2 meshes

Tassels are simple to make. Thirty 6-inch strands are held behind the mesh and the ends brought to the front by passing around the side and down through the mesh [*figure 9-3*].

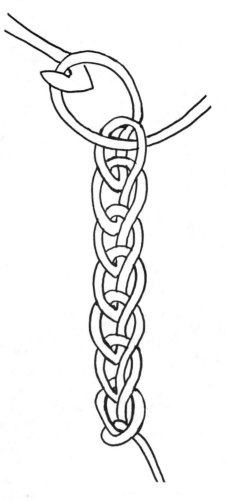

Figure 9-2. Crocheted chain.

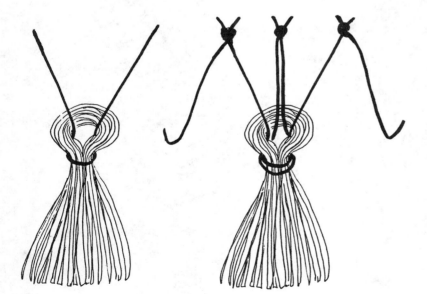

Figure 9-3. A simple tassel. Left: looped through one mesh. Right: looped through two meshes.

FLY NET BONNET

Use 1-inch, 2-inch, and 4-inch mesh boards and #9 or #12 cotton or nylon twine. Work in new-fashioned netting (page 27).

The woven band on the bonnet is 32 inches long and an inch wide with 30 one-inch loops, an inch apart, along each side.

Run a dowel through the loops on one side of the woven band and hang it from wall-mounted hooks. Begin with the 2-inch mesh board and work across the lower loops of the center band. turn the work as you complete each row.

Row 1. Net across the 30 foundation loops of the center band.

Row 2. Net 3 meshes. Tie off twine. Skip 2 meshes, then tie on twine again and work across row.

Row 3. Net across 25 meshes. Tie off twine. Skip 2 meshes. Tie on twine again and work across row (remaining 3 meshes).

Figure 9-4. Fly net bonnet.

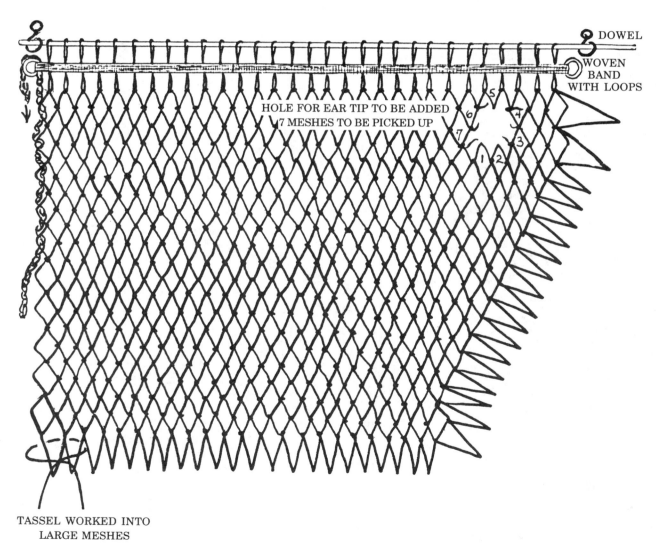

DOWEL

WOVEN BAND WITH LOOPS

HOLE FOR EAR TIP TO BE ADDED
7 MESHES TO BE PICKED UP

TASSEL WORKED INTO
LARGE MESHES

Row 4. Net 3 meshes. Tie off twine. Skip 2 meshes. Tie on twine again and work across row.

Row 5. Net across row, adding 2 meshes (see page 30, Widening) when you reach the point where meshes were skipped in the 2 previous rows.

Row 6. Make one decrease (page 30, Narrowing) at the beginning of the row. Net across remaining meshes. You should end on the same side of the net as the 2-mesh hold formed earlier.

Row 7. Net across row and make a decrease at the end of the row.

Rows 8 through 18. Continue netting, decreasing one mesh in each row—at the beginning on even rows, at the end on odd rows.

Rows 19 and 20. Net across with no further decreases.

Row 21. Change to the 4-inch mesh board. (If you do not have a mesh board this large, use the 2-inch board and wrap the lead twine around twice.) Work across the bottom edge as usual, then continue up along the tapered side to the top. Tie off.

Turn the work and net the other side to correspond to the first, making sure that the decreases are symmetrical. Tie off.

For the ear tips, return to the spaces left at rows 2, 3, and 4 [*see figure 9-4*]. These are worked with the 1-inch mesh board.

1. Tie on the twine at the edge of one ear hole and net 2 meshes into every loop around the hole. You will have 14 meshes.

2. Net 10 rows in a spiral fashion, as described in the instructions for Bait Bags (page 46).

3. Next row: decrease in every mesh.

4. Decrease again in the next row. End and tie off.

5. Work the second ear piece the same way.

Tassels (described above) decorate the tips of the ear pieces and the lower edge of the bonnet. Two of the large meshes are pulled together for each tassel.

Like the body fly net, the bonnet is held on by a crocheted chain. Approximately 40 inches long, this chain is inserted across the back of the bonnet at row 11, passing up and over the top and down to row 11 on the other side. Foot-long ends are left for tying under the horse's neck. The ear pieces hold the front of the bonnet in place, and some bonnets also have small rings sewn onto each end of the woven band for extra ties, if needed.

Nineteenth-Century Decorative Netting Patterns

One of the treasures of my library is *"The Young Ladies' Journal" Complete Guide to the Work-Table*, a century-old British book with fascinating examples of fancy-netting patterns that are both beautiful and historic. It is rare to find netting patterns drawn in such detail. Netters kept notes of

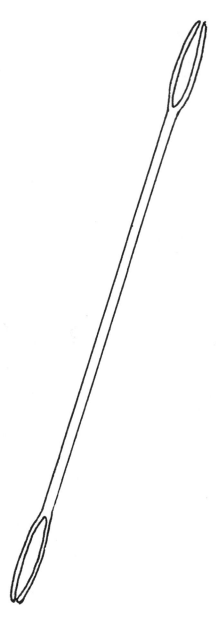

special patterns, but unfortunately most of these have been lost or discarded as the art of fancy netting declined in popularity. With the resurgence of interest in all types of fine handcrafts these days, perhaps fancy netting—and its cousin, guipure lace—will join bobbin lace and macramé as a rediscovered art.

The majority of the illustrations reproduced here are simply examples of intricate netting techniques, not instructions for finished pieces. These fancy patterns were intended to be adapted to delicate pieces such as doilies, runners, shawls, lace insets for blouses and collars, evening bags, and a variety of other decorative uses. **All are made with the new-fashioned netting method** (see page 27), for they use a very fine mesh.

Don't attempt these delicate meshes without first practicing on some of the simpler, larger-meshed projects on the preceding pages. You should be well-acquainted with new-fashioned netting before trying the complex variations that follow. I'd also recommend using a firm cotton twine for your first fancy-netting projects before attempting anything made from silk, wool, or linen. The smooth-surfaced cotton will allow you to see the knots more clearly.

Although the "Andalusian wool," "ice silk," and "Berlin wool" mentioned in the *Complete Guide to the Work Table* are items from the past and no longer (to my knowledge) available, many of these patterns may be made from today's crochet cotton, embroidery floss, or fingering yarn.

In the following directions, knitting "pins" (an archaic term for knitting needles) were used in place of mesh boards. The sizes given are British, not American. A size 14 in Great Britain corresponds to U.S. size 0 or metric 2; a British size 13 to U.S. size 1 or metric 2.5; a British size 12 to U.S. size 2 or metric 2.75; British 12 to U.S. 3 or metric 3. Actually, mesh size is entirely up to the netter, so the needle sizes given can of course be varied according to the texture you desire.

Don't be confused by the use of the term *mesh* in these facsimile pages. Throughout the rest of *Down East Netting*, I use the word to mean the actual diamond or square formed by the knotted twine. **In the following text, however, what modern netters call the mesh is referred to as the stitch, and the word mesh refers to the mesh board (or, in this case, the knitting needle used in place of a board).**

Originally, a narrow open-ended needle was used for fancy netting, but these are no longer commercially available, as far as I know. To make netting as fine as originally intended in the *Complete Guide to the Work Table,* one would have to fashion a homemade open-ended needle like the one shown here from a piece of heavy wire or a narrow strip of wood. However, there is no reason why the patterns cannot also be made on a larger scale with heavier yarn, though of course they would not have the delicacy of the originals. In any case, the patterns are fun to try, and they help one to appreciate the intricacies of this historic decorative art.

The second part of this facsimile section tells how to make guipure netting, which is, in effect, netting combined with lacemaking. In this case the netting is plain: a fine square-meshed net forms the base for fancy patterns filled in later with a needle. Decorated panels of guipure lace were often hung in Victorian front-door windows, stretched taut so the design (anything from fleurs-de-lis to peacocks) would stand out clearly.

NOTE: In pattern No. 4 of "Fancy Netting", last sentence of paragraph 1 should read, " . . . continue working as for Row 4 until desired length is reached."

NOTE: For "Fancy Netting" patterns 24, 26, 27, the increase in "stitch" (mesh) size must be done gradually in order for the circle to lay flat. Take the size used for the first row of stitches, double it for the second row, and triple it for the third row. Continue increasing at this rate until the center part of the circle is the desired circumference.

In the version shown here, the pattern changes at Row 9: six *smaller* stitches are worked into each large stitch from Row 8. As you continue to work around the circle, again increase the stitch size with each row by switching to larger and larger mesh boards (knitting needles) or by wrapping the twine around the mesh board more than once.

For the last row, two small stitches are worked into each stitch from previous row so that the perimeter of the circle will lay flat.   —B.M.

COMPLETE GUIDE TO THE WORK-TABLE

FANCY NETTING.

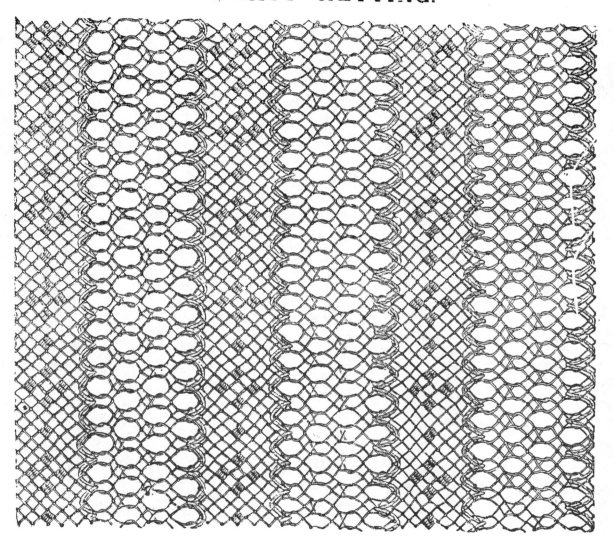

ROSE-NETTING WITH DARNED STRIPE.

DESCRIPTION OF DESIGN ON PAGE 121.

ROSE-NETTING.

This design is suitable for curtains, antimacassars, shawls, &c. It consists of stripes of rose-netting worked according to the directions given for No. 8. Four patterns of rose-netting are alternated with six rows of plain netting. The plain stripes are darned (see design).

Please read pages 105–7 before starting any of these antique patterns.

FANCY NETTING

INTRODUCTION.

NETTING has been practised for so many years that the date of its invention is unknown. Specimens of netting are still to be seen among Egyptian relics in some of the Continental museums, together with the tools that made them, and are said to be 3,000 years old. Mentions of it are made in the Bible. In the thirteenth century it appears to have been introduced into England, and has been known under the different names of caul-work, net-work, lacis, and Réseau, &c. That it can be, and is, put to many useful purposes is well known. Fishermen's nets are generally of their own make; and the more industrious of the craft spend many of their leisure hours in both making and mending their nets. Netted articles of attire were made of rich silk and gold thread; and about fifty years ago netted window-curtains were quite a fashion. It is quite probable that a turn in the wheel of fashion will bring back into special favour work that has for some years past been very little practised; although it is never entirely put aside, as the guipure netting, which is of a much more elaborate description, has been much used for window-curtains, antimacassars, drapes, trimming, &c. For the tools employed in netting, and the description of the stitches, we refer our readers to our Guipure netting.

No. 1.—COMMON NETTING.

This is the most ordinary and simple form of netting, and only differs from the mode of square netting in this respect: the work is begun by netting the number of stitches needed for the whole length of the work, and netting into them in the following rows. The stitch is precisely the same as described for square netting, page 20. No. 1 is worked with one thread for all but the lower row, where two threads are introduced to form the edge.

No. 2.—MODE OF WORKING A NETTED FOUNDATION WITH HOLES FOR EMBROIDERING TREFOILS IN.

The ground may be worked in ordinary slanting netting, or in the round netting shown in No. 3. The pattern is formed by leaving off and turning round in the middle of the rows. This pattern consists of three little holes which are afterwards worked round with flossette to form a trefoil pattern. No. 2 shows this in an increased size in order to show more clearly the mode of working the pattern. Work a plain row for the required length.

1st Row: Net five stitches, draw the needle out, turn the work, and then go back as far as the beginning of the row, making one knot in each stitch; then, returning, having arrived at the last of the five stitches, loop the thread for a long stitch on the next stitch of the upper plain row.

Then work on for five more stitches in the same way as for the first five stitches, work back, then loop the working thread round the large stitch lying on the left, as shown in No. 2, in this manner forming the first line of holes. All the returning stitches are indicated in No. 2 by dots, so that the course of the work may be easily followed; therefore the next plain row and the succeeding row forming the two holes for the trefoil need no explanation; there are four rows between each pattern row.

No. 3.—ROUND-NETTING.

This netting only differs from the common netting in the mode of placing the needle into the stitches of the preceeding line. For this, put the needle through the loop without changing the place of the finger or loop, turn the needle round and put it into the stitch of the preceeding line from above downwards, as shown by the arrow in No. 3, the working thread must remain on the right hand of the needle, and the stitch is then firmly drawn up in the usual manner. By this means the stitches in the preceeding row are a little twisted, and a round-looking stitch is formed.

No. 4.—LOOP-NETTING.

Work two rows of ordinary netting on a knitting-pin, No. 12 (Walkers' Bell Gauge). In the third row work two stitches into one, twist the thread twice round the pin. Repeat for the required length.

4th Row: Work two loops into the long-stitches of last row, twist the thread twice round. Repeat to the end of the row, and continue working only the fourth row.

No. 5.—DIAMOND PATTERN IN ROUND NETTING.

The number of stitches for this pattern is five, and one over.

1st Row: Work four stitches as described for round netting (No. 3). Work one long stitch by twisting the thread twice round the pin. Repeat for the length required.

2nd Row: Two long stitches, * three round stitches, one long stitch into the centre of first long stitch, one long stitch into next round stitch. Repeat from *.

3rd Row: One long stitch, * two round stitches, one long stitch into next long stitch, one round stitch into next long stitch, one long stitch into next round stitch. Repeat from *.

4th Row: two round stitches, one long stitch, one round stitch, one long stitch. Repeat from beginning of row.

5th Row: One round stitch, * two long stitches, three round stitches. Repeat.

6th Row: Three round, * one long, four round. Repeat from *.

7th Row: One round, * two long, three round. Repeat from *

8th Row: Two round, * one long, one round, one long, two round. Repeat from *.

9th Row: One long, two round, one long, one round. Repeat from the beginning of the row.

10th Row: Two long, three round. Repeat.

Now continue working from the first row.

Please read pages 105–7 before starting any of these antique patterns.   **111**

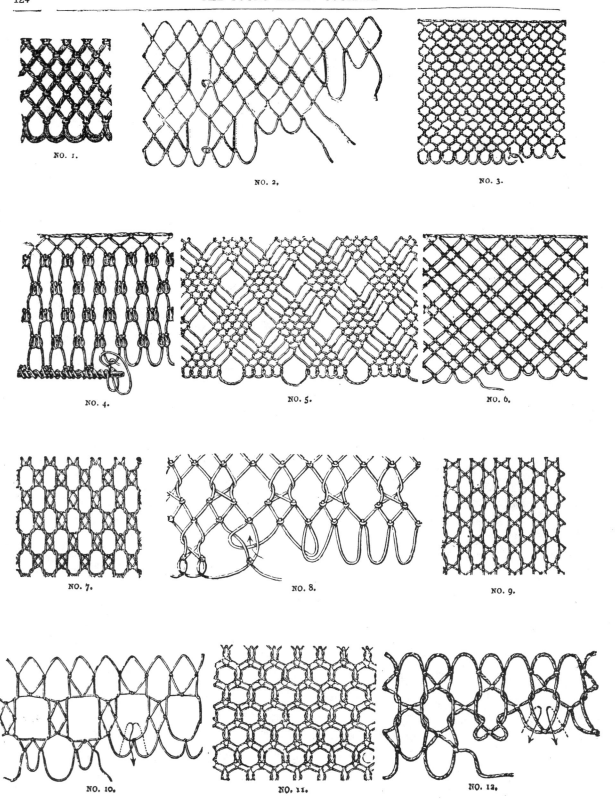

NO. 1.

NO. 2.

NO. 3.

NO. 4.

NO. 5.

NO. 6.

NO. 7.

NO. 8.

NO. 9.

NO. 10.

NO. 11.

NO. 12.

    Please read pages 105–7 before starting any of these antique patterns.

NO. 13.

NO. 14.

NO. 15.

NO. 16.

NO. 17.

NO. 18

NO. 19.

NO. 20.

NO. 21.

NO. 22.

Please read pages 105–7 before starting any of these antique patterns.   113

No. 6.—SQUARE PATTERN.

For this pattern :—
1st Row : Work one plain row.
2nd Row : One ordinary stitch, and twist the thread twice round for the large square. Repeat to the end of the row. The first and second rows are repeated alternately. Arrange the stitches so that a long stitch always comes under a short stitch.

Nos. 7 and 10.—CROSS-NETTING.

1st Row : Plain netting.
2nd Row : Net alternately one long and one common stitch.
3rd Row : Work entirely in short stitches, which naturally draw unevenly.
4th Row consists alternately of long and short stitches ; but instead of working them in the usual way, draw a stitch of last row through the long loops of the second row and net it, draw the following stitch through the same loop and net it ; continue to work a long and short stitch alternately in this way through the row. Repeat the third and fourth rows alternately.

Nos. 8, 11, and 21.—ROSE-NETTING IN PLAIN AND STRIPED VARIETIES.

No. 8 shows the detail of the work. No. 11, rose-netting ; and No. 21, rose-netting, with ribbon velvet run in at each fifth pattern, and the rose-netting is darned with silk or wool of a contrasting colour to the netting. This pattern would make very pretty shawls netted with white Andalusian wool, darned with pink, maize, or blue silk, and narrow black ribbon velvet run in.
Another variety of this design is illustrated on the cover of this Supplement.
1st Row : Net quite plain over a mesh about a third of an inch in width.
2nd Row : Net over a knitting pin (No. 12), thus : First draw the first long loop through the second and net it, then draw the second long loop through the first and net it. Repeat throughout the row. No. 8 clearly illustrates the mode of working this row. The first loop is shown drawn through the second ready for netting, at the lower middle of illustration, and the arrow represents the needle inserted ready for working the second loop.
The first and second rows are repeated alternately for the required length, looping the stitches so that the pattern is reversed.

Nos. 9 and 12.—STAR-NETTING.

Cross and star netting very much resemble each other ; after working the cross, little difficulty will be found in working the star-netting.
1st Row : One double and one plain stitch alternately with knitting pin No. 12.
2nd Row : Net plain with a mesh a third of an inch wide.
3rd Row : Draw one stitch of second row through long loop of first row, net it with a short stitch, draw the next loop through the same long loop of first, and net it with a long stitch (i.e., cotton twice round the mesh). Repeat the second and third rows for length required.

No. 10.—See No. 7.

No. 11.—See No. 8.

No. 12.—See No. 9.

No. 13.—STRIPE-NETTING.

This requires an even number of stitches.
1st Row : Net a plain row.
2nd Row : Miss the first stitch, net the second, then the first, and so on till the end of the row.
These two rows form the pattern.

No. 14.—HONEYCOMB-NETTING.

An even number of stitches are needed for this pattern.
1st Row : Plain netting.
2nd Row : Net the second stitch, then the first, next the fourth, then the third ; work thus to the end of the row.
3rd Row : Plain.
4th Row : Net a plain stitch ; begin the pattern by netting the third stitch, then the second, next the fifth, then the fourth ; end with a plain stitch, and continue to the end of the row. Repeat from first row.

No. 15.—DIAGONAL-NETTING.

The looping of the stitches is clearly shown in the design ; work with one size mesh throughout. Work a plain row.
1st Row : Work two loops into each stitch of the row.
2nd Row : Draw the second loop through the first in the direction of the arrow ; the a is drawn through b (see right of illustration). The first stitch is worked in the loop marked a ; the second in the one marked b. To mark the pattern and make it easier, the stitches drawn through might be drawn a little longer than the others. Of the two following stitches still hanging free, that marked a is the one through which the first stitch is to be made ; besides the letters the point of the arrow shows the course of the stitches. The second row is repeated throughout. To keep the stitches in the right direction, cross them by drawing them through from left to right in each alternate row.

No. 16.—BORDER : PLAIN, HONEYCOMB, AND ROSE NETTING.

1st Row : Plain netting with small mesh.
2nd Row : Work four plain stitches ; work four loops into the fifth stitch. Repeat to the end of the row.
3rd Row : Work three plain ; work the clusters of two loops together. Repeat from the beginning of row.
4th and 5th Rows : Plain.
6th Row : Like second row, beginning with two plain stitches to alternate the position of the clusters.
7th Row : Like third row, working the clusters in their proper places.
8th and 9th Rows : Plain.
Five rows of honeycomb pattern like No. 14 are now worked ; the rows are alternately of fine and coarse material, or of silk and wool to give effect to the pattern.
Work three rows plain netting.
Two patterns of rose netting ; and for the edge one row with a larger mesh and the two strands of the working material. The scallop design is worked with a needle with silk two or three times thick.

No. 17.—INSERTION : ROSE AND PLAIN NETTING EDGED WITH CROCHET.

Work four rows of plain netting with a small mesh.
One pattern rose-netting as described in No. 8.
Four plain rows.
For the edges work two double crochet stitches into each stitch of the netting.

Nos. 18 AND 19.—NETTING FOUNDATION INTERLACED WITH A NEEDLE AND THREAD.

The foundation consists of plain rows of netting worked with a contrasting colour or material from end to end; the mode of working is too clearly illustrated to need description. The pattern is varied by each row being worked in No. 18, and alternate rows being worked in No. 19.

Nos. 20 AND 22.—TRIMMINGS.

or No. 20 work five rows plain netting over a knitting-pin (No. 12). Work two patterns of star-netting as described in Nos. 9 and 12. Work two plain rows. Work one row with a mesh half an inch wide, passing over one stitch of last row. For the last row work over the large mesh into every stitch. A row of darning-stitch is worked in scallops at each edge of the star patterns. No. 22 shows a variation of the same pattern, working more rows over the small mesh, and omitting the edge row described for No. 20.

No. 21.—See No. 8.

No. 22.—See No. 20.

No. 23.—TRIMMING: NETTING.

With thread of two sizes work four rows plain over a knitting-pin (No. 14).
5th Row: With coarse thread and a half-inch mesh work into every alternate stitch of the row.
6th Row: With fine thread and small mesh work two stitches into each stitch of previous row (see design).
7th to 9th Rows: Plain netting.
10th Row: Like fifth row.
11th Row: Like sixth row.
12th to 14th Rows: Plain.
15th Row: Same as fifth row.

Nos. 24, 26, AND 27.—DOILY: NETTING.

No. 24 shows the mode of beginning a circular piece of netting, the first row of which is worked over a thread as shown in No. 26. When the row has the required number of stitches the thread must be tied as shown in the centre of No. 24. Meshes of graduated sizes are used, as shown in No. 24 and in the centre of No. 27, where seven rows of graduated sizes are worked. In the eighth row of doily a fan pattern is made by working six stitches into one of the previous row over the largest mesh. Eleven plain rows are next worked over the second, and each of two larger sizes of pins used as the meshes for the centre of doily in order to make the work flat. Next work three patterns of rose netting over meshes of three sizes. A plain row with the smallest mesh, working two stitches into one of the previous row, finishes this doily. The leaf pattern over the fan pattern is darned in.

Nos. 25 AND 28.—MODE OF BEGINNING A CIRCLE.

Make a loop, net one stitch into it, remove the mesh, net one stitch into the last, continue working rows of single stitches until you have the number required (you will find that the piece worked has the appearance of two rows of loops), pass a piece of cotton through the loops at one side, then tie the cotton, work into the loops at the other side in a circle. The increase for the circle shown in No. 25 is made by netting two stitches into each alternate stitch of the first round; in the next and following rounds always net two into the made stitch of the previous round,

this keeps the increase rows even and forms a kind of star. The clusters are worked like those described in No. 16.

Nos. 26 AND 27.—See No. 24.

No. 28.—See No. 25.

No. 29.—FOUNDATION WITH NEEDLEWORK PATTERN.

This design consists of rows of ordinary netting with crosses worked with a needle and thread into each alternate square; the mode of working the cross will be easily seen in the design; the thread is carried from square to square by twisting it round the right-hand foundation thread.

No. 30.—OPEN-WORK AND DARNED STRIPE.

Work seven plain rows over a small mesh.
8th Row: With a mesh a size larger work one stitch into each stitch of previous row.
9th Row: With the same mesh net two stitches together throughout.
10th Row: Net two stitches into one throughout. Repeat from the beginning of the pattern.
The darning is worked with wool or silk of a contrasting colour (see design).

No. 31.—TRIMMING, WITH THICK LOOPS AND FAN EDGE.

Work two rows plain netting.
3rd Row: Work three stitches into one of previous row, one stitch into each of two successive stitches. Repeat throughout the row.
4th Row: Plain working through the clusters of three stitches together as one stitch.
5th Row: Plain.
6th Row: Like third row, working the clusters of three stitches between those of the third row.
7th Row: Like fourth row.
8th Row: Work into two stitches together below the clusters of sixth row, work one into all the other stitches.
9th Row: Work over a mesh rather more than half an inch in width four stitches into one stitch of last row, pass over three stitches, and repeat.
10th Row: With the mesh first used work one stitch into each of the four worked into one stitch, take the next loop, pass it through the centre of the three stitches passed over in the previous row, work one stitch into it. Repeat from the beginning of the row.
The mode of passing the long loop through the centre of the three stitches is clearly shown by the thin line in the design.

No. 32.—LOOSE LOOP PATTERN.

1st and 2nd Rows: Plain netting.
3rd Row: Two plain loops, place the working thread as usual over the mesh, and pass the needle close over the nearest knot of the last row but one from underneath perpendicularly, put the thread round the mesh again, and let the needle go again through the same stitch from underneath upwards, and then work a common stitch in the next stitch of the last row so that the thread is put three times round the mesh as shown in the lower right hand corner of illustration. Repeat from the beginning of the row.
4th and 5th Rows: Plain.
6th Row: Like third row, working so that the clusters of loops come between the clusters of third row.

NO. 24.

NO. 23.

NO. 25.

NO. 29.

NO. 30.

NO. 26.

NO. 27.

NO. 28.

NO. 31.

NO. 32.

Please read pages 105–7 before starting any of these antique patterns.

COMPLETE GUIDE TO THE WORK-TABLE.

....

FANCY NETTING.

NOS. 33 AND 34.—LAPPETS.

Please read pages 105–7 before starting any of these antique patterns.   117

DESCRIPTION OF DESIGNS ON PAGE 129.

LAPPET FOR CAPS, &c.

No. 33.—This lappet is composed of one stripe of the open work and darned stripe shown in illustration 30, (page 128), edged by a fan pattern.

To form the point at the end, tie the cotton into the first of the four loops, work one stitch into each of the other four stitches, turn, knot the cotton into the centre of last loop without working over a mesh, one stitch over the mesh into each of the three next loops, turn, knot the cotton into the first loop in the same way as last, one stitch into each of two loops, turn, knot the cotton into the first loop, one stitch into the next.

Now work a row round both sides and the end.

1st Row: In loop netting described for the stripe, working quite round the end and along the other side.

2nd and 3rd Rows: Plain netting.

4th Row: Over the larger mesh work one stitch into a loop, six stitches into the next loop, and repeat.

Over the small mesh work one stitch into each stitch of last row.

No. 34.—This is in sheaf pattern, with bunches of loops. The sheaf pattern is described in No. 39 of this Supplement. Make a foundation of as many loops as you require for the length of lappet.

1st Row: Plain over a mesh the eighth of an inch in width.

2nd Row: Sheaf netting, leaving one of the long loops without tying into a sheaf; for the end on one of these commence the 3rd Row: Work over the small mesh, ten stitches into it, one stitch into each of the stitches worked with double cotton. Now work the 4th Row all round plain.

5th Row: In the loop netting described for the stripe of No. 1.

6th Row: Plain.

7th Row: Bunches of loops described in No. 4 of this Supplement.

8th Row: Plain.

Please read pages 105–7 before starting any of these antique patterns.

FANCY NETTING (*Continued*).

No. 35.—SCALLOP.

These scallops make a pretty edge for curtains, antimacassars, &c.; they are worked separately and sewn to the curtain, or whatever they are intended to ornament, with a needle and thread.

1st Row : Over a mesh three-quarters of an inch wide work twenty-seven stitches.

2nd Row: Work with double thread and knitting-pin No. 12 for a mesh, one stitch into each stitch of last row.

3rd to 5th Rows : Like second row, but with single instead of double cotton.

6th Row : Rose netting, with coarser cotton, directions and illustrations for which will be found in Nos. 8 and 11, (page 124).

8th to 10th Rows : Like third to fifth rows.

9th Row : With double thread over the large mesh, one stitch into each stitch of last row.

10th Row : One stitch into two loops together. Repeat to the end of the row.

Draw up the first row of loops with a needle and thread (see design).

For the crochet heading, one double into last loop of tenth row, seven chain, one double treble into rose netting, seven chain, one double treble into fourth row, seven chain, one double treble into long loops, three chain, one quadruple treble into the centre of cluster of loops, three chain, one double treble into long loop, seven chain, one double treble into fourth row, seven chain, one double treble into rose netting, seven chain, one double treble into tenth row.

No. 36.—BORDER WITH DOUBLE LOOSE LOOPS.

This will form a pretty border for neckerchiefs worked in Ice silk. After the foundation, which may be in plain netting, work with double silk over a mesh one-eighth inch in width.

1st and 2nd Rows : Plain.

3rd Row : Five plain, one loose loop (loose loops were described in No. 32, page 127), five plain. Now you must begin each row from the same side.

4th Row : One plain, one loose loop, six plain.

5th Row : Three plain, one loose loop, one plain, one loose loop, three plain.

6th Row : Plain.

7th Row : Two plain, one loose loop, three plain, one loose loop, two plain, repeat.

8th Row : Plain.

9th Row : One plain, one loose loop, two plain, one loose loop, two plain, one loose loop.

10th Row : Plain.

11th Row : One loose loop, seven plain, repeat.

12th Row : Take a half-inch mesh, work three stitches in each loop of last row.

13th Row : Take a knitting-pin No. 14. Work one stitch in each stitch of last row.

14th Row : Like thirteenth over the thick mesh.

15th Row : Over the thick mesh net six loops together each time.

No. 37.—FAN NETTING.

This kind of netting is used for edgings, stripes, &c.

1st and 2nd Rows : Plain netting over a quarter-inch mesh.

3rd Row : Cotton twice over the mesh for each loop.

4th Row : Plain netting.

5th Row : Five stitches into one stitch of previous row, cotton twice over the mesh, pass over one stitch, and repeat.

6th Row : One stitch into each of four loops worked into one loop, pass over the long loop, and repeat.

7th Row : One stitch into each of the three loops of last row, cotton twice over the mesh, pass over the next loop, and repeat.

8th Row : One stitch into each of the two loops of last row, cotton twice over the mesh, pass over the long loop, and repeat to the end of the row.

No. 38.—BORDER WITH BUNCHES OF LOOPS.

This forms a pretty border for shawls, curtains, &c. It is worked throughout with double cotton or double Andalusian wool, and a half-inch mesh.

1st Row : Plain netting.

2nd Row : Two plain, one bunch of loops.

Each bunch of loops is worked in the following way : After a common stitch, which must be rather long, put the thread again loosely round the mesh and push the needle through without making a knot, then make another stitch-knot so that two loops remain in the same stitch. As shown in the lower right corner, the loop bunch is fastened here, for which the needle is carried from behind round the bunch and pushed in front from underneath through the loop, and is drawn up tightly ; now work one plain, one bunch of loops.

3rd Row : One plain, three bunches of loops separated by one plain stitch.

4th Row : Like second row.

5th Row : Like third row.

6th Row : Like second row.

7th and 8th Rows : Plain.

9th Row : Three plain, one bunch.

10th Row : Like second row.

11th Row : Like third row.

12th Row : Bunches of loops throughout.

13th Row : One stitch into each plain stitch of last row.

No. 39.—EDGING : DOUBLE FAN OR SHEAF.

This forms a pretty edging for doilys, night nets, &c.

1st to 3rd Rows : Plain netting over a quarter-inch mesh.

4th Row : With a mesh an inch wide, and double cotton, work one stitch into each loop.

5th Row : With the small mesh one stitch into each loop. The long-stitches are caught together in clusters of three by a needle and cotton ; each stitch must be firmly fastened at back and cut off. The heading is worked in crochet ; one double into a stitch, three chain, and repeat to the end of the row.

NO. 35.

NO. 36.

NO. 37.

NO. 38.

NO. 35

NO. 69.

NO. 41.

Please read pages 105–7 before starting any of these antique patterns.

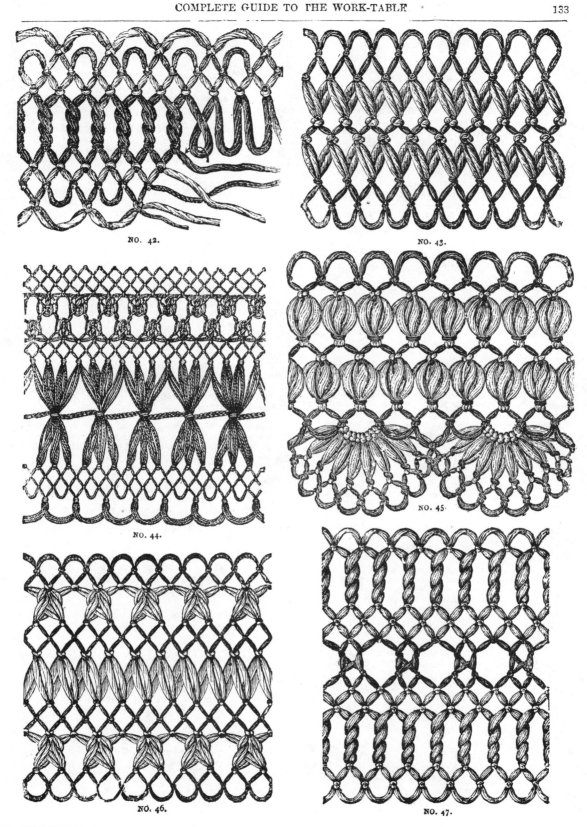

NO. 42.

NO. 43.

NO. 44.

NO. 45.

NO. 46.

NO. 47.

Please read pages 105–7 before starting any of these antique patterns. **121**

No. 40.—BORDER WITH ROUND-LOOP HEADING.

This design will make a pretty shawl or neckerchief, netted with Ice silk and Andalusian wool, and two round meshes one half the size of the other; the plain netting with the silk and round loops in wool. The three rows would be repeated any number of times to form the foundation.

1st Row: Work with double wool and the large mesh, one stitch into each stitch of foundation, in the same way as described for round netting, No. 3, (page 123).

2nd and 3rd Rows: Plain netting with a small mesh.

4th Row: Like first row.

5th and 6th Rows: Like second and third rows.

7th Row: With double wool, and a mesh three-quarter inch wide, work three stitches into a loop, pass over one loop, and repeat.

8th and 9th Rows: With the small mesh and single silk plain netting.

10th Row: With the largest mesh and double wool one stitch into a loop, one through the next loop and that already worked into together (see arrow), and one stitch into the second stitch, pass over one stitch, and repeat to the end of row.

11th Row: With the small mesh and single silk, one stitch into each loop of last row.

No. 41.—DIAMOND PATTERN.

This design is suitable for foundations of shawls or stripes for clouds, antimacassars, &c.

1st Row: Plain.

2nd Row: Work two loops into a stitch, draw the next loop rather longer, and repeat to end of the row.

3rd Row: One stitch into each loop of last row.

4th Row: Work a stitch through two loops together under the two loops worked into a stitch in second row. Repeat to the end of the row. Repeat from the first row. The double loops are worked across with a needle and cotton, as shown in the upper part of illustration.

No. 42.—DESIGN WITH TWISTED LOOPS.

This design is worked in wool, and is suitable for shawls, antimacassars, &c.

1st and 2nd Rows: Plain over a mesh one-third of an inch in width.

3rd Row: Plain over a mesh one inch in width.

4th Row: Twist a loop twice and work through the lower part (as indicated by the arrow), one stitch into each loop over the small mesh.

5th and 6th Rows: Like first and second rows.

7th Row: With wool of two colours one stitch into a loop over the small mesh, turn the wool twice over the mesh, pass over one loop and repeat.

The work is to be taken from the foundation, the knots picked out, and a row like the sixth worked into the first row.

No. 43.—STRIPE FOR SHAWLS, &c.

This design is worked with wool.

1st and 2nd Rows: Plain over a small mesh.

3rd Row: With a mesh double the size and double wool, one stitch into each stitch of last row.

4th Row: With the small mesh and single wool, plain netting.

5th Row: Like third row.

6th and 7th Rows: Like first and second rows.

No. 44.—BORDER: ROSE AND SHEAF PATTERN

1st to 3rd Rows: With a knitting pin No. 11 for a mesh work in plain netting :—

4th and 5th Rows: Rose netting (see page 128).

6th and 7th Rows: Plain.

8th Row: With treble cotton and a mesh rather more than an inch in width work one stitch into each loop.

9th to 11th Rows: With the small mesh and single cotton work one stitch into each loop.

12th Row: In round netting (for which see Illustration 3, page 124) work with double cotton one stitch into a loop, cotton twice over the mesh, pass over one stitch, and repeat.

The sheafs are caught together by crochet. Work one double over three triple loops, seven chain, repeat. A double length of cotton is darned in a straight line above and below the two rows of rose pattern.

No. 45.—BORDER WITH TUFTS AND SCALLOPED EDGE.

This border is suitable for woollen shawls; it may be worked with Berlin wool of two colours.

1st Row: Plain netting with the dark shade over a quarter-inch mesh.

2nd Row: With the light shade over a half-inch mesh work three stitches into one loop, draw the next loop very tightly, and repeat to the end of the row.

3rd Row: One stitch through the three loops together over the small mesh. Repeat to the end of the row.

4th Row: Like second row.

5th Row: Like third row.

6th Row: One stitch into each loop of last row.

7th Row: Over the large mesh and with the light shade eight stitches into one loop, wool twice over the mesh, pass over three loops, and repeat to the end of the row.

8th Row: With the dark shade and the small mesh one stitch over the long loop of last row into the second of the three stitches passed over, one stitch into each of the other loops.

9th Row: One stitch into each loop of last row.

Take the work from the foundation, pick out the knots, work with the dark wool and the large mesh one stitch into each loop.

No. 46.—DESIGN: LONG AND CROSSED LOOPS.

This design is worked with knitting silk and Andalusian wool.

For the 1st and 2nd Rows: work in plain netting with silk and a mesh measuring a quarter of an inch in breadth.

3rd Row: With double wool and a half-inch mesh work two stitches into one loop, one stitch into each of the two next loops. Repeat from the beginning of the row.

4th Row: Take the long loop at the left of a short loop, pass it through the short loop, and net it with silk and the smaller mesh; take the next long loop and pass it through the same short loop and net it. Repeat to the end of the row.

5th Row: One stitch into each loop of last row.

6th Row: With double wool and the large mesh one stitch into each loop of last row.

7th and 8th Rows: With silk and the small mesh, like fifth row.

9th and 10th Rows: Like third and fourth rows.

11th Row: Like fifth row.

Please read pages 105–7 before starting any of these antique patterns.

No. 47.—BORDER: CROSS NETTING AND TWISTED LOOPS.

1st and 2nd Rows: With a quarter-inch mesh one stitch into each loop.

3rd and 4th Rows: Twisted loops as described for the third and fourth rows of No. 8.

5th Row: One stitch into each loop.

6th and 7th Rows: Cross netting. Cross netting was described in Nos. 7 and 10, page 124.

8th and 9th Rows: One stitch into each loop.

10th and 11th Rows: Like third and fourth rows.

No. 48.—NECKERCHIEF.

MATERIALS REQUIRED: 1¾ oz black silk, a knitting-pin No. 12 (Walker's gauge), and a half-inch ivory mesh.

Begin the neckerchief in the centre from point to point upon a foundation of 112 stitches, working over the smaller mesh two plain rows, but do not work the last stitch of each row.

3rd Row: Work over the large mesh with double silk one stitch into each loop except the last; do not work that.

4th Row: With the small mesh and single silk work one stitch into each long loop, twisting the loops as described in No. 42, page 133; continue to repeat from the second row until you have worked eight repeats of the pattern; take the work from the foundation, pink out the knots, run a thread through the second row, and work upon the first row; for the second half as described for the first, commencing with the row of long twisted loops.

For the border :—

1st Round: Over the small mesh net one stitch into each stitch of foundation, except in the stitch at each end of the first row; in these work two stitches.

2nd Round: Like first round.

3rd Round: Over the large mesh work four stitches into one stitch of previous round, pass over one stitch. Repeat all round.

4th and 5th Rounds: Over the small mesh, one stitch into each stitch of last round.

6th Round: Like third round.

7th Round: With double silk one stitch into each stitch of last round.

No. 49.—FRINGE.

This fringe may either be worked with wool or cotton.

1st Row: For the foundation, plain with a small mesh.

2nd Row: Over a three-quarter inch mesh, with double cotton or wool, one stitch into each loop.

3rd Row: Over a knitting-pin No. 13 net one stitch into the second loop, pass the first loop at the back of the second, and net it. Repeat, crossing the loops in this way throughout the row.

3rd Row: Like second row.

4th Row: Net one loop into the first, pass over the second, net into the third, pass the second at the back of third and net it, continue to cross the loops to the end of the row. Netting the first stitch plain in alternate rows causes the crossed loops to come between the upper row of crossed loops.

5th Row: Over a quarter-inch mesh net one into each loop of last row. Cut lengths of cotton or wool, and knot eight strands into each loop of last row.

No. 50.—DESIGN FOR ANTIMACASSARS, FICHUS, &c.: DARNED NETTING.

The foundation is netted plain over a knitting pin No. 14; any number of rows may be worked.

For the border :—

1st Row: Work two stitches in each loop of foundation over a quarter-inch mesh

2nd Row: Over the small mesh work one stitch through the second stitch worked into one loop of last row, and into the next loop together, so that the double loop always slants to the right.

3rd Row: Plain.

4th Row: One stitch over the large mesh into a stitch of last row, pass over one stitch, six stitches into the next, pass over one stitch and repeat.

5th Row: One stitch over the large mesh into each stitch of last row.

6th Row: With the small mesh work into each loop of last row, twisting the long loops as described for No. 42, (page 134). The pattern is darned in the foundation with soft knitting cotton.

No. 51.—TASSEL FRINGE.

Make a foundation with Berlin wool over a knitting pin No. 10 (Walker's gauge).

Work six plain rows.

7th Row: Net one into each stitch with double wool over a mesh two inches in width, cut all the loops in the centre, take two strands from each of two loops, bind them once round with silk of the same colour as the wool, take three strands of wool two and a half inches in length, bind them in with the strands of the loop, fasten the silk securely, and cut off.

Now bind the tassel round about a quarter of an inch below the last binding, comb out the wool, and cut the edges even for the tassel.

NETTED MITTEN.

Six or seven skeins of fine netting silk or black twist are needed for a pair of mittens; and for the mesh use knitting pins Nos. 13 and 14 (Walker's bell gauge), and a small steel netting needle. Work twelve rows of diagonal netting (shown in No. 15, page 126). Net fifty rows plain netting on the smaller mesh; then work two patterns of honeycomb netting (No. 14, page 126). This completes the arm, which join up; and net round one plain row.

2nd Round: Increase by netting two stitches in one twelfth and fourteenth stitches to begin the thumb, the rest of the round is plain netting. Increase two loops to form the thumb in each of the two loops already mentioned in each alternate round for eighteen rounds.

To finish the thumb, net round about ten rounds on the stitches of the thumb, and finish with a little fan pattern made by netting six stitches into one loop of previous round, pass over one loop, one stitch into the next, pass over one loop, and repeat. This round should be worked over a quarter-inch mesh. In the following round work one stitch into each loop of preceding round, using the small mesh.

Now continue to work upon the hand until it is as long as you desire, and finish with the fan pattern given for the top of the thumb. Both hands are worked alike, as there is no right or wrong side until you darn a pattern on the back of the hand, which may be of stripes, diamonds, or any design you please.

NETTED NIGHT-NET.

This night-net is particularly recommended to persons who suffer from headache, as it keeps the hair closely together without any pressure on the head.

MATERIALS REQUIRED: Crochet cotton No. 4, netting-needle, and mesh about quarter-inch wide.

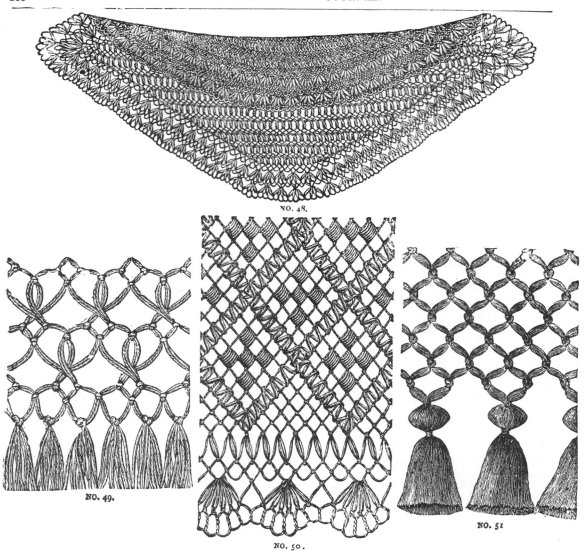

NO. 48.

NO. 49.

NO. 50.

NO. 51

Commence with twenty-two stitches, and net backwards and forwards fifteen rows, and then take out the foundation thread, draw it through the middle of the oblong. Now work round and make one knot in each stitch of the preceding row; there must be eighteen rows netted round, or more if not large enough; then follows the broad row for the ribbon to pass through. For this take a half-inch mesh, or put the cotton twice round the small mesh at every stitch. After this broad row work two rows over the first mesh, then follows the narrow lace for the outer edge; for this, net one row over the broad mesh, making always five knots in one stitch, passing over the next stitch. Now take again the small mesh, and pass over again in each row the same stitches that were passed over in the first row, whilst in the rest one stitch must be made in each stitch of preceding row until there is only one stitch to work, and the next to pass over alternately.

This ends the lace.

Draw a ribbon through the broad row of netting, and tie it at the back, and sew on the bow at the top.

NETTED CURTAINS.

Netted curtains are generally preferred made of square netting. To begin, you must work as for the square and oblong netting described in Nos. 10 and 13, in page 22. The size of cotton will of course rule the size of the mesh and the quantity of cotton required. Evans' (Boar's Head cotton), about 0000, will make a nice curtain, worked quite plainly, and edged with a fancy border in netting or a row of ball fringe.

For a coarser curtain, Strutt's knitting cotton No. 10, mesh, knitting-pin No. 10 (Walker's bell gauge). A curtain about three yards and a-half long would require 350 stitches. This could be worked with rows of plain netting, and any of the fancy stripes which we have illustrated and described in our Fancy Netting Supplements. The rose and plain pattern shown on page 121 will make very beautiful curtains worked in Strutt's crochet cotton No. 12, with a mesh knitting-pin No. 12 (Walker's bell gauge).

[THE END.]

COMPLETE GUIDE TO THE WORK-TABLE.

GUIPURE NETTING

FULL DIRECTIONS FOR

GUIPURE NETTING.

Please read pages 105–7 before starting any of these antique patterns.

DESCRIPTION OF ILLUSTRATION ON PAGE 17.

SQUARE IN GUIPURE NETTING.

This square is suitable for mixing with squares of another pattern in netting, or with squares of other material, for chair-backs, counterpanes, bassinette-quilts, &c. The square shows a number of the most elaborate stitches used in guipure netting. As these can only be learned by a study of the various stitches contained in these Supplements, the following hints will be all that are needful here :—The close flat-stitch embroidery worked upon the foundation covered with point de toile must be worked before the guipure in relief. Buttonhole-stitch completes the inner part of the embroidery to make the edge appear even.

    Please read pages 105–7 before starting any of these antique patterns.

GUIPURE NETTING.

—∘∘⦙∘∘—

INTRODUCTION.

THIS beautiful work has long been fashionable, and the varied purposes for which it can be used, its strength and durability, will continue to keep it fashionable for many years to come. These Supplements are a revise of those given some years since with this Journal, with additional directions and illustrations for netting foundations; and as our "Complete Guide to the Work-table" would not answer to its name were these omitted, we trust those ladies who have preserved the original issue will be pleased to see these in a form which will enable them to have them bound with the rest of the Supplements forming the "Complete Guide to the Work-table."

Some of the uses to which the work can be put we will enumerate:—For household purposes: window-curtains, toilet-covers, toilet-cushions, antimacassars, and doilys. For articles of dress: parasol-covers, borders for handkerchiefs, caps, cravats, chemisettes, collars, cuffs. Insertions and lace of all widths for trimming underlinen; and also, worked fine and in the more elaborate patterns, the lace can be used for trimming dresses of the richest material, such as velvet, satin, &c.

Guipure Netting, Guipure d'Art, Filet Guipure, and Filet Brode are one and the same work, which has gone under a great many more names since its introduction in the middle ages. The word "Guipure" comes from *Guipé*—a kind of thick cord or thread, round which threads of gold, silver, and silk were twisted.

IMPLEMENTS REQUIRED.

Netting-needles and meshes of various sizes. These are made of steel for fine work, and of ivory, bone, and boxwood for larger and coarser work. The needles must be chosen of a suitable size for the mesh—not too large, or they will be difficult to get through the work; and not too small, or they will not hold enough of material without joining in frequent and perhaps inconvenient parts of the foundation. A good stirrup is requisite if a lead cushion is not at hand, as it is very needful to keep the work firm. The lead cushions are shown in the next page. We consider the lead cushion has an advantage over the stirrup, as ladies need not stoop to their work. We will, however, give directions for a good stirrup for those who may prefer to use one. Linen thread is the material used for the foundation and for the stitches of guipure netting. A wire frame is also essential for working in. Care must be taken to have the working material quite smooth and even, without knots. The proper thread and implements for guipure netting are supplied by Mr. Bedford.

Nos. 1 AND 2.—TO FILL A NETTING-NEEDLE.

Tie a little loop over one of the forked ends, and wind the thread from end to end firmly on the needle; when the needle is filled press the prongs together quite close. For very fine netting, which will not admit the filled needle through the holes, a long blunt darning-needle must be used.

No. 3.—NETTING-MESH.

For fine work knitting-pins are generally used for meshes; but for larger work boxwood, bone, and ivory meshes; both flat and round are sold at all fancy-work shops.

To know the size mesh you should use, you must measure one side of a square, and select a mesh the exact size of it.

STIRRUP.

We have elsewhere stated that we consider the weighted cushion better than a stirrup for netting, as it prevents the need of stooping over the work, which is desirable; but there are ladies who have so accustomed themselves to work with a stirrup, that they find it more convenient than the cushion, therefore we insert the following directions for a very good stirrup:

MATERIALS: A pair of wood or bone pins, No. 12; two small pieces of scarlet worsted braid.

Cast on nine stitches, knit three rows plain.

3rd Row: Knit two together throughout the row.

4th Row: Slip the first stitch, * take up the loop between the stitches and knit it, knit a stitch, take up the loop, &c., from * to the end of the row.

5th Row: Plain knitting.

6th Row: Purl.

The third, fourth, fifth, and sixth rows are to be repeated sixteen times; work the plain rows as at the commencement.

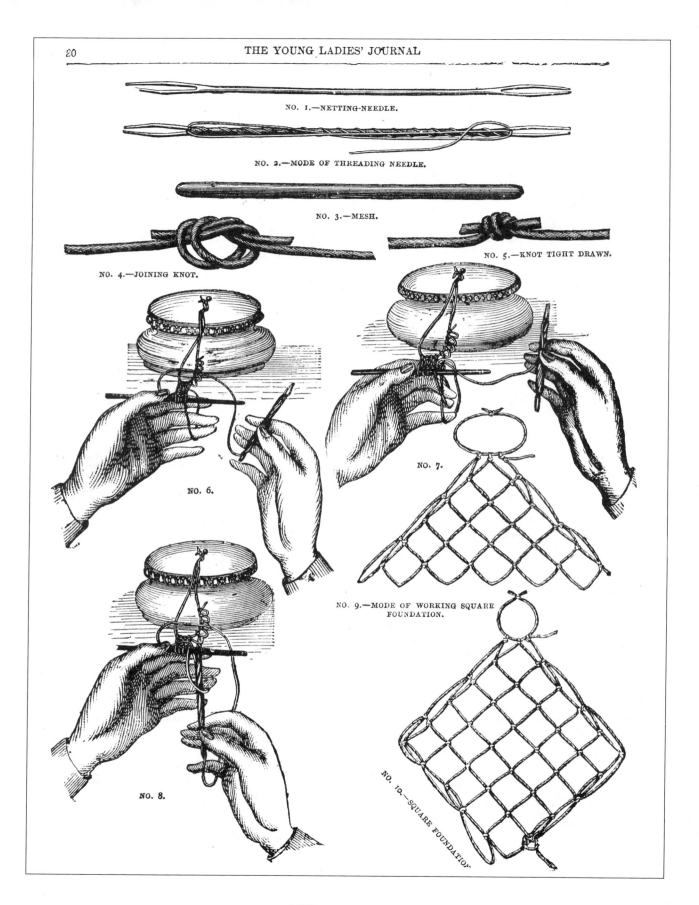

NO. 1.—NETTING-NEEDLE.

NO. 2.—MODE OF THREADING NEEDLE.

NO. 3.—MESH.

NO. 4.—JOINING KNOT.

NO. 5.—KNOT TIGHT DRAWN.

NO. 6.

NO. 7.

NO. 8.

NO. 9.—MODE OF WORKING SQUARE FOUNDATION.

NO. 10.—SQUARE FOUNDATION.

Please read pages 105–7 before starting any of these antique patterns.

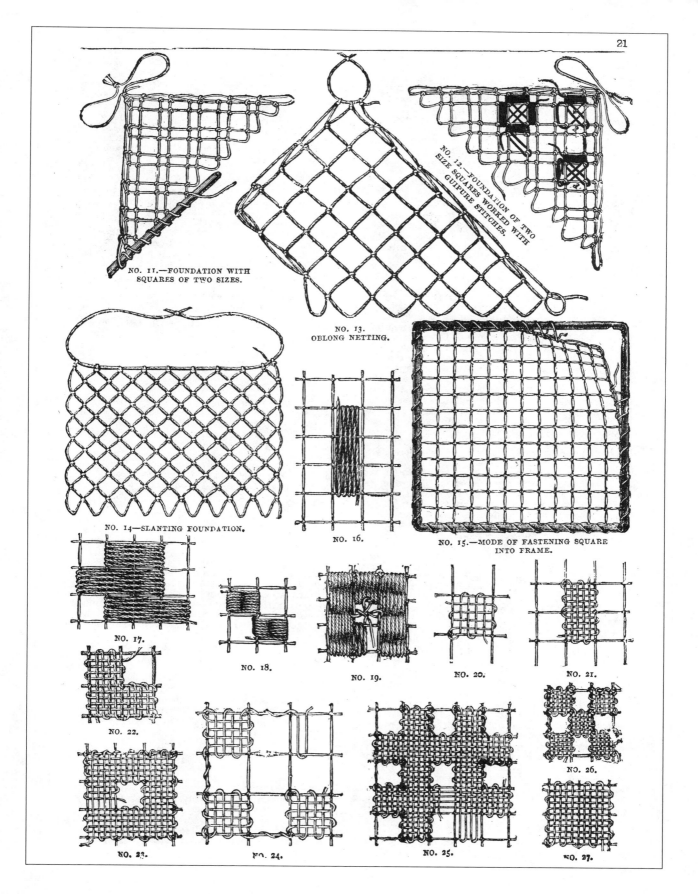

NO. 11.—FOUNDATION WITH
SQUARES OF TWO SIZES.

NO. 12.—FOUNDATION OF TWO
SIZE SQUARES WORKED WITH
GUIPURE STITCHES.

NO. 13.
OBLONG NETTING.

NO. 14.—SLANTING FOUNDATION.

NO. 16.

NO. 15.—MODE OF FASTENING SQUARE
INTO FRAME.

NO. 17.

NO. 18.

NO. 19.

NO. 20.

NO. 21.

NO. 22.

NO. 23.

NO. 24.

NO. 25.

NO. 26.

NO. 27.

Please read pages 105-7 before starting any of these antique patterns.   129

Cover a thin piece of wood three inches long with ribbon or silk of the colour of the braid, and line the braid with ribbon; then sew the knitted ends to the ribbon covering the wood. To make a foundation to net upon, net two or three stitches, and continue until you have a piece about a yard long, which you can net upon at any part suitable to the length of your work. The two ends of the foundation can then be fastened together to the top of the stirrup.

Nos. 4 and 5.—KNOT FOR JOINING.

The knot represented in No. 4 needs no description, being simply the usual knot-loop with the two ends placed over each other, firmly drawn (see No. 5) and the ends cut off. This knot is considered as secure as the complicated weaver's knot.

Nos. 6 to 8.—DIRECTIONS FOR NETTING.

The foundation: Netting,—is commenced in various ways. We recommend a piece of thread tied in a knot and fastened to a heavy cushion, as shown in Nos. 6 to 8, which forms a foundation for the first row. When the work is finished the thread is taken out.

Take the thread-loop, fasten it to the cushion, tie the working-thread to the loop, take the filled needle in the right hand and the mesh in the left; hold the latter horizontally between the thumb and forefinger, as shown in No. 6; lay the working-thread over the mesh downwards round the middle finger of the left hand, and then between the mesh and the forefinger, a little towards the left, where the left thumb encloses the thread, and by that means the loop laid round the mesh and finger is firmly held; then, according to No. 7, the needle is carried again towards the right, and pushed from underneath through the thread-loop lying round the left hand, forming a wide scallop with the thread; then the needle is placed under the loop, and between the finger and mesh again through the foundation-stitch; keeping the left hand quite still, draw the needle quite through with the right hand; then with the help of the left hand draw the knot quite tight, which completes the stitch. This is done by taking the two middle fingers of the left hand out of the loop in taking up the needle with the right hand (see No. 8), and only directing the knot to the top of the mesh with the right hand, where all the knots are placed in a line close together. The loop must be quickly and firmly drawn up with the little finger of the left hand over which the thread is carried slowly—and by that means the stitches are evenly drawn up. It is better, if possible, to avoid making knots except at the outer-side stitches. Having once learnt the stitch, netting a ground presents no difficulty, as the stitches are all worked like those of the preceding row. When the whole line is finished the mesh is carefully taken out, the work turned round, and the mesh placed again to commence another row, which is worked in the same manner. Every stitch is commenced by pushing the needle into a stitch of the preceding line. After refilling the needle a knot must be tied, as shown in Nos. 4 and 5, and as before explained.

Nos. 9 and 10.—SQUARE NETTING.

For netting in straight lines, begin always at one corner with two stitches, and work rows forwards and backwards. At the end of each row increase one stitch by making two stitches in one at the last stitch until the netting is the required width. No. 9 shows the commencement of the corner. The straight netting is either in squares, in an oblong form, in stripes, or in angular edges.

For the square: Work as many holes in the length as in the breadth, increasing at the end of each row until there is one stitch more than the finished square of holes must contain in one line. For the five holes of the square represented in No. 10, there must be six stitches; then net one more row over this with the same number of stitches plain, and decrease in the same proportion, for which the two last stitches in each row must be netted together with one knot.

Having by this means reduced the number again to two, unite the two last stitches with one knot in the middle. This is, however, no stitch; simply carry the thread tight across to the joining knots.

Nos. 11 and 12.—SQUARE FOUNDATIONS OF TWO SIZES.

These foundations are made by putting the thread once round for the small hole, and twice for the large hole of the square. No. 12 shows the style of work for which this foundation is required.

No. 13.—OBLONG NETTING.

For an oblong form or shape, as shown in No. 13, the increasing for the corner must be continued until there are two more stitches than are required for the breadth. This increasing must be continued without interruption on one side; but on the opposite side it will be necessary always to decrease, so that the number of stitches always remains the same. When the netting is the required length, the last corner must be worked by decreasing, as in the square.

No. 14.—SLANTING NETTING.

For the slanting netting, commence with the requisite number of stitches for the length, and work rows forwards and backwards, as shown in No. 14. These slanted stripes are used for collars, cuffs, cravat-ends, the separate gored parts of parasol-covers, &c., and in all cases where there is a deviation from the square, and where the foundation has to be cut. In this case work the separate parts in the whole foundation rather close to each other, and cut them out of each other, and fasten the outlines with buttonhole-stitch.

No. 15.—WIRE FRAME FOR GUIPURE NETTING.

For the guipure work the netted foundation must, for small things, be placed in a strong wire frame soldered by a tinman. It must be large enough to stretch the work tightly. No. 15 shows the work nearly placed in the frame, and ready for the darning, which must be done carefully, and the threads evenly drawn. The wire frame is covered with a narrow sarsnet ribbon, to which the work is sewn (see Illustration).

CIRCULAR FOUNDATIONS.

Circular foundations for doilys, circular cushions, mats, &c., are worked precisely the same as square netting. The circle must be formed by running a thread round to the size required, and working over it with close buttonhole-stitch. Cut away the superfluous part.

Please read pages 105-7 before starting any of these antique patterns.

COMPLETE GUIDE TO THE WORK-TABLE.

GENERAL REMARKS ON GUIPURE NETTING.

The size of the cotton must be regulated by the holes of the netted ground, so as to blend nicely, and to be neither too close nor too loose.

Generally the same size of thread may be taken as that used for the foundation; sometimes the pattern requires different parts to be worked with different cotton—some fine, some coarse. A common darning or tapestry needle may be used. Very nice needles are made for the guipure work without points. The greatest care and accuracy are required in working all stitches in guipure; the thread must be always carried alternately over and under the netted threads; the work must always be uninterrupted, and the thread fastened with a firm knot (see Nos. 4 and 5); and when it is impossible to pass immediately from a filled-up part to the next hole of the netted ground, the thread must be wound round the threads between that and the next hole, to be worked as carefully as possible, so as to be almost imperceptible.

Nos. 16 to 19.—POINT DE REPRISE: DARNING-STITCH.

This is a stitch which is employed in nearly all patterns; in some it is used alone, in others alternated with other stitches. The principle of the stitch is that of ordinary darning.

The holes must be entirely filled up, placing the needle over one thread of the netting and under the other. The darning must be always in the same direction. Any deviation in the pattern will be seen in the designs. We can give no description of these stitches which could be half as useful to the worker as a careful observation of the Diagrams Nos. 16 to 19.

Nos. 20 to 27 and 32.—POINT DE TOILE: TRELLIS-WORK STITCH.

In working this stitch great care must be taken to make the threads cross each other evenly. Different patterns may be worked in this stitch. The number of threads in a square must be regulated by the size of the square; but there must be the same number of long and cross threads, and the numbers must be even—two, four, six, &c.; an odd number of threads would spoil the work. All the designs show where the patterns commence and where the thread is wound round to continue the pattern.

Nos. 28 to 30, and 33 to 35.—POINT D'ESPRIT: FESTOON-STITCH.

Work rows forwards and backwards. In this pattern the alternate over and under stitches are not regularly observed, but by attention to the designs the deviations may be seen and the stitch easily worked. Sometimes the whole netted ground is covered with this stitch.

No. 31.—ANGULAR EDGE FOR HANDKERCHIEF-BORDERS, &c.

For an angular edge round pocket-handkerchiefs, covers, or the outer edge of a square with a thick middle piece of linen, &c. (see No. 31), it is advisable to place the design before one. The commencing corner may be easily known by the commencing thread which forms the upper point of the square. Beginning with a corner, increase until there are two more than double the number of stitches that are required for the breadth; therefore, for the edge of square No. 31, which is three stitches broad, eight stitches will be required. Then the part marked with dotted lines a 1 to a 2 must be worked with four stitches as far as the half of the corner; and then turning round with these stitches, continue the stripe, always increasing at the outer and decreasing at the inner edge. For the next corner at the inner edge, where until now the decreasing has been carried on, following the row marked b 1 and b 2, after the decreasing, make one more stitch in the outermost edge stitch, and with this begin the increasing for the second side of the inner edge; at the outer edge decrease in the same proportion. Having arrived at the third (the opposite one to the beginning) corner, cut off the thread at the last row at the inner edge (see c 1 to c 2) according to the knot d 1, the thread is then put on again at the upper corner; and according to the dotted line the first row of the side edge as far as d 2 is to be worked. The work is then continued as at the first half of the edge as far as the under corner, and on arriving there the thread is again cut off at the inner side. Put the thread on afresh at the knot marked g; and, according to design, in the next row enclose the two inner stitches where the cut-off thread hangs, together with one knot which forms the corner, and must now be completed as for a square by decreasing at the end of each row. This is the last corner.

No. 32.

Is another example of point de toile. The directions for working will be found under No. 20.

Nos. 33 to 35.

Further examples of point d'esprit or festoon-stitch. No. 34 shows a ground entirely covered with this stitch. For directions for working see No. 28.

No. 36.—COMBINATION OF FESTOON AND TRELLIS STITCHES.

This design gives the festoon (point d'esprit and trellis-stitch) joined together in one pattern. The latter is worked like common darning (point de reprise).

No. 37.—COMBINATION OF TRELLIS-STITCH AND WHEELS.

The trellis-stitch has already been explained; each row of trellis should be worked first, and afterwards the rows of wheels, spun-stitches, or spider-webs, as they are sometimes called. These stitches will be illustrated and described in our next Supplement.

Nos. 38 AND 39.—COMBINATION OF POINT DE REPRISE AND FESTOON.

Each of these stitches have already been illustrated and explained. A combination of the two in fine work will make a pretty lace for trimming dresses, &c. They will also make a very pretty doily or antimacassar. If space will admit of our doing so in a future Supplement, we will give a design for these patterns in a proper size. Nos. 38 and 39 are shown in a greatly increased size to facilitate copying them. We need hardly say that the letters show where to repeat the pattern; a must meet a, and b...

Please read pages 105–7 before starting any of these antique patterns.

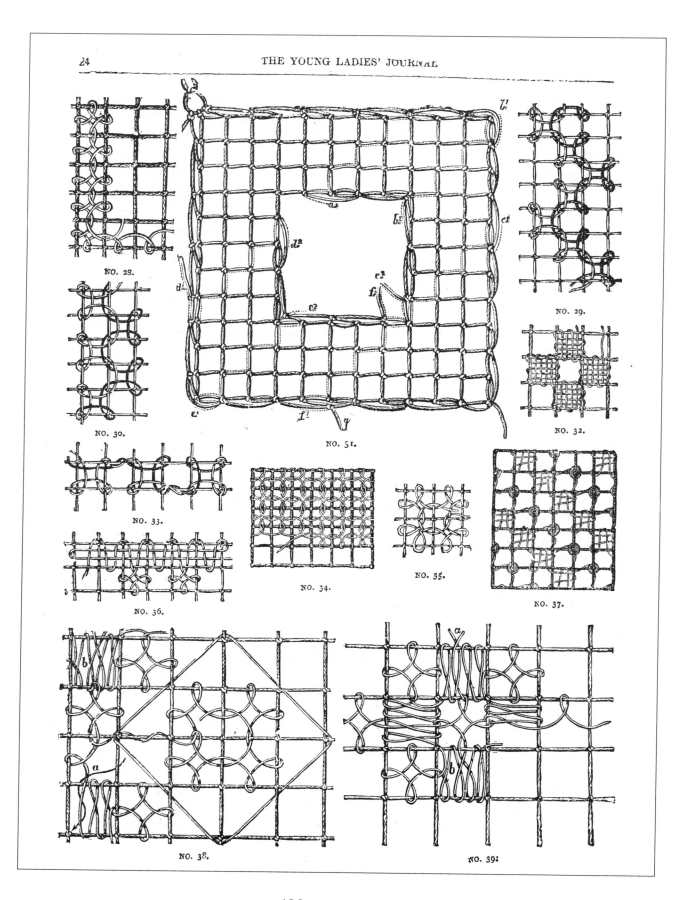

NO. 28.

NO. 29.

NO. 30.

NO. 31.

NO. 32.

NO. 33.

NO. 34.

NO. 35.

NO. 36.

NO. 37.

NO. 38.

NO. 39.

Please read pages 105–7 before starting any of these antique patterns.

THE YOUNG LADIES' JOURNAL

COMPLETE GUIDE TO THE WORK-TABLE.

GUIPURE NETTING

FULL DIRECTIONS FOR

GUIPURE NETTING.

DESCRIPTION OF ILLUSTRATION ON PAGE 25.

CRAVAT-END.

This design is worked in some of the most elaborate stitches, the directions for all of which will be found in these Supplements. The cravat-ends are finished by a pearl lace edge, which must be tacked on to the scallop of the cravat-end, and worked over with fine buttonhole-stitch. The finished ends may be tacked up a silk, net, or muslin cravat.

Please read pages 105–7 before starting any of these antique patterns.

GUIPURE NETTING (*Continued*).

—◦◦❀◦◦—

Nos. 40 to 46.—POINT CROISE: CROSS-STITCH.

These stitches may be used as a whole or half pattern for separate squares, or an entire surface with either single or double threads ; the second thread is wound round the first.

No. 40 shows the mode of working a single thread crossed with a tied knot, which fastens all the threads at the crossing - point. This stitch resembles the common buttonhole-stitch, with this difference only, that the stitch is put in over instead of next to the starting-thread.

The double-thread cross No. 41 requires the crossed thread to be once more tied in a separate hole of the square. For this double cross stretch the first loose thread for two bars of the cross lying near each other, then return as far as the middle only. Twist the thread round the latter, from here going always forwards and backwards to form the third and fourth bars ; then unite all the four bars by one stitch, and then twist the thread a few times round the first bar with a single thread and finish. After uniting the four cross-bars, it will be easy to make a little round pattern in the middle by drawing the thread round the cross. No. 42 shows clearly the mode of working half cross-stitch in rows.

No. 43 shows a simple mode of making a cross-stitch with a thread.

Work the first line of this cross-stitch by looping a simple thread cross-stitch round the thread of the netted foundation (as in working with a needle), then in the returning row, which completes the cross ; the knot must be always made in the middle.

Twisted crosses may be made in the same manner by first stretching the single thread across, and then twisting the thread round in returning. This is clearly shown in No. 44, with little round patterns added at the cross points (spinning patterns), by working round the tied knots in the twisted lines.

The next variation of the cross-stitch, which also forms the ground of the spun-stitch, and which is the thread-cross interwoven with the *point d'esprit* in No. 45, may also have a loose thread circle as in No. 46.

The interwoven cross of No. 41 may now be completed by the *point d'esprit*, for which stick always through the winding of the cross-bars, as shown in No. 45.

———

Nos. 46 to 49.—SPINNING-STITCH AND WHEELS.

These patterns are generally worked over four holes of the netted square at the crossing-point of the cross-bars stretched across, and either unite the eight radii or meet over these in the centre of a netted hole with the thread wound round. This winding round is so contrived that the wound bars lie underneath the threads of the foundation, and the stitch is on this account called a web. No. 46 represents one of these patterns with a loose thread circle ; No. 47 a web with a looped circle, and it forms the middle of the pattern represented in No. 50. A wheel differs from a web in the mode of weaving it ; in the former the threads appear to be reversed.

No. 49 represents a finished wheel surrounded with very pretty picots.

———

Nos. 50 and 51.—PICOTS.

These picots consist of buttonhole-stitches worked close together, as shown in No. 50. The number of

THE YOUNG LADIES' JOURNAL

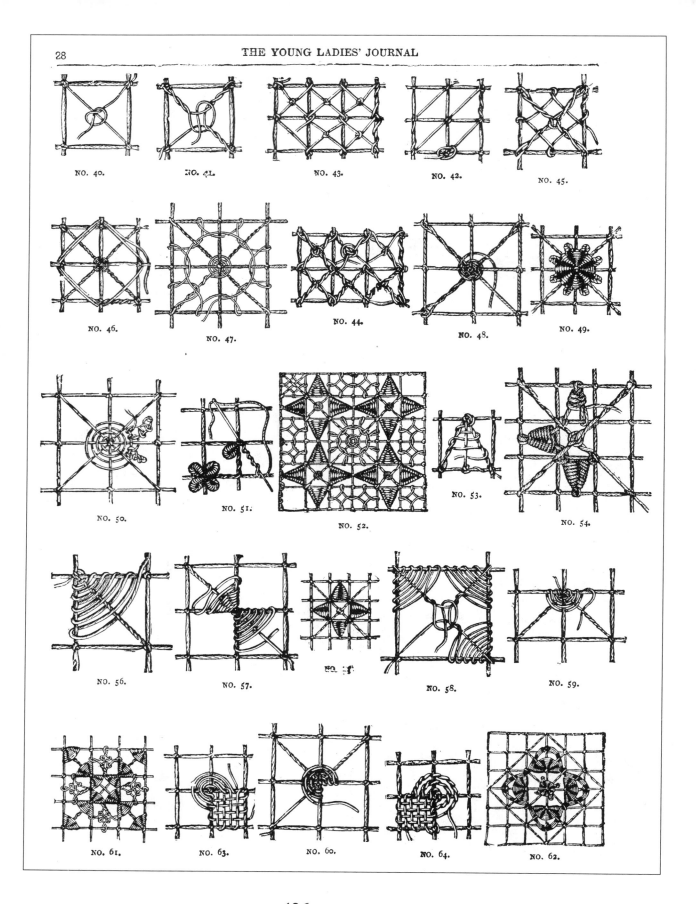

NO. 40.   NO. 41.   NO. 43.   NO. 42.   NO. 45.

NO. 46.   NO. 47.   NO. 44.   NO. 48.   NO. 49.

NO. 50.   NO. 51.   NO. 52.   NO. 53.   NO. 54.

NO. 56.   NO. 57.   NO. 55.   NO. 58.   NO. 59.

NO. 61.   NO. 63.   NO. 60.   NO. 64.   NO. 62.

Please read pages 105–7 before starting any of these antique patterns.

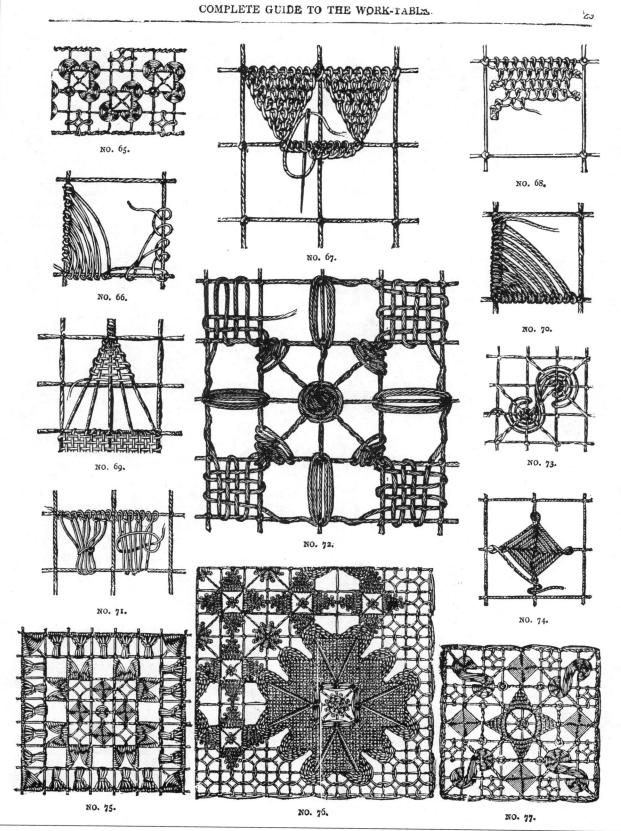

NO. 65.

NO. 66.

NO. 67.

NO. 68.

NO. 69.

NO. 70.

NO. 71.

NO. 72.

NO. 73.

NO. 74.

NO. 75.

NO. 76.

NO. 77.

Please read pages 105–7 before starting any of these antique patterns.   137

buttonhole-stitches must be regulated by the quality of the cotton and the size of the picot.

No. 51 shows another very effective picot, which may be worked either round the threads that cross each other in the netting for the middle of a cross (cross-stitch), or round a little spinning-stitch or wheel ; this kind may also be used for flowers. These twisted picots are worked in the well-known *broderie à la minute* (see No. 51). For this kind of picot make first a buttonhole-stitch round the netted cross, push the needle in it, and wind the cotton ten or twelve times round for one picot ; then carefully draw another buttonhole-stitch round the netted cross to fasten the finished picot and to prepare for the next.

———

Nos. 52 TO 55.—PYRAMID-STITCH.

This stitch is made with sometimes one, two, or more divisions.

No. 52 gives a design with patterns of pyramid-stitch in three divisions, which are worked according to No. 53. This stitch differs only so far from that in two divisions, in that from the middle hole when the triangle is stretched across, the thread stretched across is carried to the middle of the netted bar, and rises from there to the point.

No. 54 shows the mode of working this. Tie the thread on with a knot, carry it as far as the middle of the outer netting thread of the pattern, fasten it for a triangle again to the middle hole returning.

By winding the last thread backwards the point of the pyramid is again reached, and the bars must now be closely worked in point de reprise, as shown in the design.

No. 55 shows a little finished pattern with one division between the bars of a web.

These pyramid-stitches may be made stronger and more effective by twisting several stretched threads together, which form a kind of frame.

———

Nos. 56 TO 58 AND 61.—MUSHROOM-STITCH.

This is worked in a kind of point de reprise in a corner of a netted square, a twisted thread having been previously drawn across obliquely (see No. 56).

Nos. 56 to 58 show the usual modes of placing these patterns together. No. 61 gives a little square pattern containing double point d'esprit between the different arrangements of the mushroom-stitch.

The double point d'esprit is merely a second worked inside the first.

———

Nos. 59 AND 60, 62 TO 65.—POINT EVANTAIL : FAN-STITCH.

This is a kind of continuation of the mushroom-stitch, and may be easily worked from Nos. 59 and 60. Nos. 62 and 65 show how they may be arranged in patterns. The flat fan-stitch in No. 59 forms an almost exclusive pattern of itself, but the corner fan-stitch in No. 60 serves also as a finish to the trellis-work parts, as shown in Nos. 63 and 64. A variety of

this pattern is called the twisted fan-stitch, and answers the same purpose, as shown also in a square pattern in No. 76.

———

Nos. 66 TO 70.—SCALLOPS.

These are numerous in their arrangement and modes of working. In order to make two of these pointed scallops in a hole of the netting, work always two buttonhole-stitches on the thread of the netting intended for the long side of each scallop (according to No. 66), one buttonhole-stitch on the thread intended for the short side of the scallop at the middle point of the threads turned towards the star, so that the latter seems only half filled when the side thread is covered with stitches. No. 66 shows one scallop with loose threads finished ; the second laid on. Having finished the latter, carry the thread at the foot of the finished scallops as far as the next disengaged hole to work the next two scallops, or by means of a bar of the thread cross in the middle of the star ; continue the work.

The thick button scallops (Nos. 67 and 68) are worked in rows forwards and backwards in common buttonhole-stitch, as shown in No. 67. For thick buttonhole scallops with picots, see No. 68.

The thick pyramid scallop is like the pyramid-stitch, but according to No. 68, it lies loose upon the ground, and the frame of stretched threads is worked in point de reprise. In working these large scallops, in which the threads are closely interwoven, and which has the effect of pyramid-stitch in five divisions, it is very necessary that the five threads of the frame should be firmly stretched. They all unite in the point—not together round the knots of the netted foundation, but after the looping are placed perpendicularly on the straight netted bar, and closely wound round. This twisted bar may be completed with a thick pattern, spun-stitch, a wheel, or a picot. The threads on the foot of the frame joined to the trellis-stitch may be easily worked from No. 69. The loose corner scallop which serves for filling up this, as well as the slanting half of a hole of the netting in the mushroom-stitch, is worked the same as No. 70, without a supporting middle thread, and like the loose star scallop worked with buttonhole-stitch in No. 66. For every triangle two buttonhole-stitches must be made over each thread of the netting.

———

No. 71.—TUFTED BUTTONHOLE-STITCH.

This stitch will be very easily worked from the design. It forms the border to the square No. 75.

———

No. 72.—OBLONG PATTERN.

These patterns are formed by drawing the thread loosely round the netting. They are used for ornamenting larger patterns. No. 72 shows how they are used with other stitches to form a pattern.

Please read pages 105–7 before starting any of these antique patterns.

No. 73.—THE LETTER "S" STITCH.

This is a sort of combination of the mushroom-stitch, and is used in square No. 77.

———

No. 74.—THICK SQUARE.

This simple stitch needs no description—it will be seen in the finished square No. 77.

———

Nos. 75 AND 77.—SQUARES IN GUIPURE NETTING.

These squares may be used alternately, and will make a pretty insertion, a heading for guipure lace, or joined for pincushion-tops, doilys, &c.

———

No. 76.—QUARTER OF SQUARE.

All the stitches in this design have been already described, except the stalk-stitch which crosses the point de toile. They are worked according to Nos. 85 and 86. This square will make a pretty doily, or, combined with other squares, will serve for antimacassars, &c.

———

No. 78.—PATTERN IN FAN, OBLONG, AND SPINNING STITCHES.

This shows the mode of working a combination of the above stitches.

———

Nos. 79 TO 81 AND 90.—STAR OR RADII.

For the mode of working the star represented in No. 79, see No. 80. The star requires cross-bars placed in the same manner as for a wheel, the ends of which must again have crossbars for the rounding of the star. Round the interwoven wheel in the middle the separate radii are arranged, which are formed, according to the previous directions, of loose threads round the bars of netting, and placed together in a bunch at the under part with two buttonhole-stitches upon the wheel. The little stars, arranged in a pretty pattern with cross-stitch and point d'esprit in No. 90, consist, as shown in No. 81, of loose threads stretched across and joined by being twice firmly interwoven in the middle.

———

No. 82.—DOUBLE CROSS.

This pattern is very effective for the middle of a square, or even for a corner. The loose threads must be first stretched across from one side over the hole of the netting, and a bar wound round in the opposite direction, interweaving it with the first bar, as shown in design.

———

Nos. 83 TO 85 AND 88, 89.—GUIPURE IN RELIEF.

These very effective patterns may be placed upon a ground of point de toile, or even upon plain netting. They present no difficulty, but require practice and the greatest accuracy. They consist of loose threads stretched over the foundation, and worked in like the point de reprise—for small patterns, over two threads, with one division; for broad patterns, leaves, &c., with two or three divisions over three or more threads. Leaves should be graduated. Stalks on leaves, or sometimes raised veins (see No. 76), are formed, according to the thickness required, of threads stretched across, wound once or several times round, and closely corded in returning. The large patterns, in filling up the stretched threads of which the frame of bars is composed, require a thread of the foundation to be worked in here and there lightly, which causes the guipure to keep its place better. No. 83 gives a finished cross in relief upon a netted foundation, covered with point de toile.

No. 84 shows the mode of working this. Nos. 85 and 89 show the mode of placing the large and small leaves and stalks so clearly that no description is necessary. No. 88 shows a combination of these stitches.

———

Nos. 86 AND 87.—BUTTONHOLE-STITCH EDGE.

The buttonhole-stitch makes a very pretty scallop border. This edge may be either plain or ornamented with picots. It is advisable to work it in a frame. It is important that it should be carefully traced, so that when the threads of the netting are cut away the stitches remain in their places.

For this stretch the thread firmly round the netted thread, and tie it always with the loop described for the cross-stitch (see No. 40). Returning it must be closely twisted again, and then fastened with buttonhole-stitch, as shown in No. 86. No. 87 shows the mode of working the picots; they are formed by simply making another separate buttonhole-stitch, which lies free underneath, and is fastened to the next in continuing the row.

———

CONCLUSION.

From the descriptions and illustrations of stitches which we have given in these Supplements we believe our readers will find no difficulty in working any of the guipure netting designs which we have already given, and shall continue to give, in our Journal. The designs on pages 17 and 25 of our Guipure Netting Supplements are each somewhat difficult, and should not be attempted until the stitches have all been well practised; but they are very beautiful designs, and show what very nice work may be produced in guipure netting.

Please read pages 105–7 before starting any of these antique patterns.

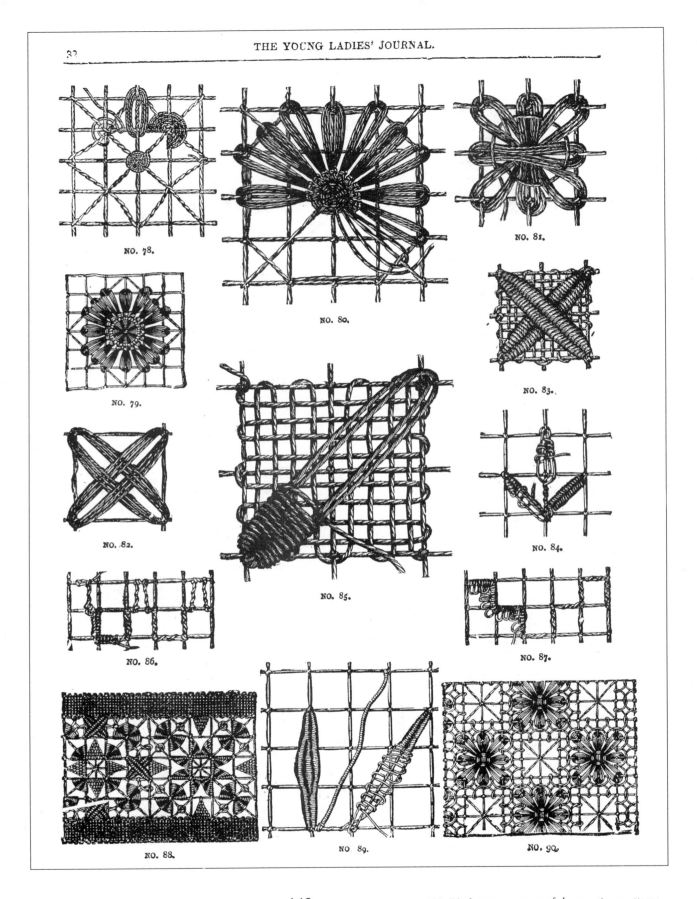

NO. 78.

NO. 80.

NO. 81.

NO. 79.

NO. 83.

NO. 82.

NO. 84.

NO. 85.

NO. 86.

NO. 87.

NO. 88.

NO 89.

NO. 90.

List of Twine Companies

Champlin Net Company
401 Front Street
Jonesville, LA 71343

Crowe Rope Company
Warren, ME 04864

Defender Industries, Inc.
225 Main Street
New Rochelle, NY 10801

Delta Net and Twine Company
P.O. Box 356
619 East Clay Street
Greenville, MS 38701

FNT Industries, Inc.
977 First Street
Menominee, MI 49858

Glavan Trawl Mfg. Co.
201 Oak Street
Biloxi, MS 39530

**Handweavers Guild of
    America, Inc.**
65 LaSalle Rd.
West Hartford, CT 06107

Marcraft Inc.
Flying Point
Freeport, ME 04032

Marinovich Trawl
Biloxi, MS 39530

**Memphis Net and Twine,
    Inc.**
2481 Mathews Avenue
P.O. Box 8331
Memphis, TN 38108

Nichols Net and Twine Co.
Rural Route 3, Bend Road
East St. Louis, IL 62201

Nylon Net Co.
615 E. Bodley Ave.
Box 592
Memphis, TN 38101

**Sterling Net and Twine Co.,
    Inc.**
18 Label Street
Montclair, NJ 07042

Bibliography

A Brief Sketch of the Town of Vinalhaven, prepared by the Town on Its One-Hundredth Anniversary. Rockland, Me.: Free Press, 1889.

Bath, Virginia Churchill. *Lace.* Henry Regnery Co., 1974 (114 West Illinois St., Chicago, IL 66610).

Blandford, P.W. *Netmaking.* Brown, Son & Ferguson, 1941, 1969. (52 Darnley St., Glasgow, S.I.).

Garner, John. *How to Make and Set Nets: The Technology of Netting.* Coward & Gerrish Ltd., 1962. (Larkhall, Bath, Somerset, Great Britain).

Gravmont, R., and Wenstrom, E. *Fishermen's Knots and Nets.* Cambridge, Md.: Cornell Maritime Press, 1948.

Gravmont, R., and Hensel, J. *Encyclopedia of Knots and Fancy Rope Work.* Cambridge, Md.: Cornell Maritime Press, 1939.

Hatch, W. H. "Islesboro Net Makers." *Down East*, March 1969, 42–43.

Klust, Gerhard. *Netting Material for Fishing Gear.* Fishing News Books Ltd., 1973 (23 Rosemont Ave., West Byfleet, Surry, England).

Lorimer, P.D. *Net Mending and Patching.* Pacific Sea Grant Advisory Prog., Oregon State Univ., 1976.

O'Farrell, R.C. *Seafood Fishing for Amateur and Professional.* London and Tunbridge: Whitefriars Press Ltd., 1971 (Fishing News Books Ltd., 110 Fleet St., London EC4 A2JL Great Britain).

Richetti, Maggie. *Universal Yarn Finder.* N.Y.: Prentice-Hall, 1987.

Tidball, Harriet. *The Weaver's Book: Fundamentals of Handweaving.* Macmillan Publishing Co., 1961 (866 Third Ave., New York, NY 10022).

Vinalhaven Wind, March 1, 1884 issue.

von Brandt, Andres. *Fish Catching Methods of the World.* Margate: Eyre & Spottiswoode Ltd., Thanet Press, 1972 (Fishing News Books Ltd., 23 Rosemount Ave., West Byfleet, Surrey, England).

Winslow, Sidney L. *Fish Scales and Stone Chips.* Portland, Me.: Machigonne Press, 1952.